T R A N S M O N T A N

Off the Highway

Published by New Star Books
Series Editor: Terry Glavin

Other books in the Transmontanus series

Off the Highway

GROWING UP IN NORTH DELTA

Mette Bach

TRANSMONTANUS ◆ NEW STAR BOOKS VANCOUVER

For my parents

The year is 1949, and the occasion is the unveiling of plans for a tunnel under the South Arm of the Fraser River. Engineer George Massey, with the pointer, is showing the location of the Deas Island Tunnel — since renamed after Massey himself — which would open in 1959, linking North Delta and Ladner to Richmond and Vancouver. At far left is John Kirkland, reeve of the city of Delta. The other two men in the photo are unidentified. DELTA ARCHIVES 2009-33-6

boonies: *The sticks, in the middle of nowhere. Usually associated with living out in the country.*

"Man, I live out in the boonies. It takes an hour and a half to get to the nearest gas station."

. . . A podunk area of the state in which usually nothing, not even shit, happens. Usually near a swampy land area — which makes it a good place to lure crabs using slabs of raw meat tied to strings and a net to scoop them up with.

"Argh! I can't believe I'm stuck out in the boonies this early in the morning."
   "Well, you agreed to join me in catching crabs which we must get started on before the sun comes up."

— THE URBAN DICTIONARY

www.urbandictionary.com

Life In the Boonies

I'm from the boonies. That's what we used to say. The boonies, for us, was some 45 minutes to an hour outside of Vancouver, a city that we hardly ever visited. There were houses and town-houses and several kilometres between bus stops. There were more gas stations than theatres; more tire specials and carpet sales than tall buildings; more empty lots than sculpted parks. There was a bowling alley, an ice rink, a second-rate mall, a third-rate mall and a public pool. To live there was to live in a place never talked about and never shown in movies or portrayed in books. To live there was to be off centre. To live there was to not exist. This was a place where people got bored and died, where people flipped houses and had Sunday barbeques. This was a place where everyone knew what was on television and nobody talked to their neighbours. This was a place where nothing special had ever happened and nothing ever would. This was a place where people still spiked their hair, where warehouses advertised inexpensive laminate flooring by painting a sign on the side of a building. This was also a place where, once in while, if you were lucky, you might see a deer gallop across the highway late at night.

We thought the boonies were all the same. We were also young and stupid.

Welcome to North Delta

If you're heading south from Vancouver, take the 84th Avenue exit off Highway 91, keep to your right and circle around an Esso gas station, a Tim Horton's, and a sports complex with ice rinks and a pub, and you'll find yourself in a big parking lot. If you park in that lot, right next to the rinks, and walk underneath the foundational pillars of the Alex Fraser Bridge, you will find a path that leads directly into Burns Bog. You'll see graffiti on the concrete, garbage littered about and faded posters advertising home repairs or new and exciting business opportunities. You'll hear the deafening din of traffic overhead from Highway 91, that relentless shroud of noise.

It might not feel like you are standing on some of the most precious land in the Northern hemisphere. You'll feel a little more bounce in your step and smell the mossy mildewy greenness but it probably won't feel spectacular. You won't mistake Burns Bog for one of Canada's natural wonders. There are no look-out points, no glossy signs and no gift shop that sells Burns Bog key chains or T-shirts. If you go to the bog, you are unlikely to run into any tourists. It takes work to go there, which is good because you shouldn't go unless you're committed and if you're committed, you may have read pamphlets or books about how to behave in bogs. This will serve you well. From time to time, you might find brochures at the entrance, pamphlets that describe bog etiquette and bog plants and animals — but it depends on whether the Burns Bog Conservation Society has the money to make photocopies and whether one of the volunteers has the time to bike down from their Scott Road office.

Once you get to the bog, there's a trail that follows a stream. If you walk along this path, you will see a boardwalk on your right. It was built by volunteers, paid for by donations, and meant for you to walk on so that you can go into the bog without disturbing the activity around you. If it is summer, you will see plentiful salal, blueberry bushes and lichen-covered cedars. You will also likely see rabbits, slugs and insects. You might spot a heron or a crane. If you concentrate, or spend enough time on that path, your ears might filter out the sounds of the highway traffic above. You might not hear it after a while or, like the animals, you will continue to hear it but you will adapt because that's what we do with constant noise.

Volunteer-built paths through Burns Bog keep visitors off the sensitive terrain.

MARK MUSHET PHOTO

People who visit or live on Canada's west coast tend to prefer rugged mountains, crashing waves and gigantic trees. That's what's on our brochures; that's what we like: bears and mountain lions, rock climbers and surfers, danger and drama. Bogs are spongy, marshy peat lands with little shrubs and little creatures. Burns Bog is not a postcard image and, with its distinct odour, it is not an idyllic hideaway from the city. In fact, if you listen carefully to the bog, it will tell you that it does not care for human visitors, that it never has. There are countless mythologies dating back thousands of years that warn people of the dangers of bogs. These cautionary tales seem to speak from the bogs themselves, whose slow evolutions do not take well to quick-paced humans nor the company we keep.

Though there were once bears in the bog, they have, for the most part, moved on and one is more likely to spot a shrew or a salamander than anything threatening. Maybe that's why the bog is a more likely destination for teenagers who live nearby and are looking for a place to roll a joint or drink a beer, or folks looking to take their German shepherd for a walk.

Within walking distance of Burns Bog there is a site that, when it was excavated in the 1970s, revealed a village that dates back to the Holocene era, some 9,000 years ago. Bone fragments and other artifacts — hooks, jewellery and arrows — suggest that this was a seasonal spot where people fished for salmon, hunted elk and deer and gathered around fires. It is also a burial ground that shows evidence of three distinct cultural periods, making the site unusual not just for the Lower Mainland or British Columbia or even Canada but for human history in general. For a while — a good three decades — it looked as though the provincial government might protect this site, known as St. Mungo (named after the patron Saint of Glasgow — it was named by a Scot, of course). There was some talk about turning the site into an official park, just as there has been some talk about building an interpretative centre for Burns Bog. The dedicated folks at the Burns Bog Conservation Society see it as crucial that we teach people about the importance of preserving peat bogs. Since most of Canada's wetlands have already been destroyed and we are, globally speaking,

Members of the Burns Bog Conservation Society have created a guided tour for visitors. Signposts provide information about the bog's flora and fauna.
MARK MUSHET
PHOTO

responsible for one fifth of what's left of our planet's wetlands, it seems that our collective survival hinges on our ability to protect such things as peat lands and 9,000-year-old villages. But some folks see it differently.

In 2008, in celebration of 150 years of European settlement on this land, British Columbia's premier, Gordon Campbell, decided it would be a great gift to the people of British Columbia to construct a beautiful new highway. The South Fraser Perimeter Road would enable traffic to flow easily between the Tsawwassen Ferry Terminal and Surrey's Port Mann Bridge.

This highway won't run *through* the peat lands, it'll run alongside them. Since 2004, most of what's left of Burns

Bog has been protected. The federal government bought the land so that developers no longer could. It was designated conservation land because it is home to hundreds of species that would have nowhere else to go if Burns Bog were turned into something else. The Prime Minister, Stephen Harper, backed Premier Campbell's highway idea and generously offered federal funding to further the road construction. They are of the belief that congestion is the biggest problem in our culture. Campbell said this on television. Stephen Harper stood behind him and nodded as the two men agreed that progress has no time for truckers to get held up in traffic.

When I heard about this highway project, I was ambivalent. Instinctively, I was concerned about the construction of a highway that would run parallel to what was being described as a unique and vulnerable nature reserve. Who wouldn't be? But in terms of my personal history with North Delta, there's a part of me that just wants it (and by extension, that time in my life) paved over. Regardless of how I felt, I knew I had an obligation to revisit and investigate what was happening in my old hood. The only problem with going back to North Delta was that it meant going back to North Delta.

Not From Around Here

When we were teens, my friends and I used to think North Delta was the most boring suburb in the Lower Mainland. We understood that "most boring" is a subjective judgment. It's hard to make comparisons between suburbs. Maybe boring is more of a continuum. Langley has outlet stores and, at the time I lived in North Delta, Langley had a drive-in movie theatre. Cloverdale has a rodeo. Ladner has farms and fruit stands. White Rock has the beach and a strip of eateries. Surrey has malls, cheap motels and a notorious reputation. Abbotsford has the air show. Chilliwack has waterslides. New Westminster has history. The only possible challenger for the "most boring" title might be Richmond but that would be wrong, too, since they have the danger factor — if there is a major earthquake, they'll likely find themselves under a metre or two of water. Even without the earthquake, Richmond has night markets and an expansive selection of restaurants,

This was Scott Road, North Delta's main thoroughfare, when the author was growing up there. DELTA ARCHIVES 2004-003-68

karaoke bars and bubble tea cafes.

Most people think of North Delta as the five exits off Highway 91, half way between Vancouver and the U.S. border. North Delta is also known for its landfill, the one thing that used to make North Delta a destination point for the rest of the Lower Mainland's trash until it ran out of room. The Lower Mainland's sewage travels through North Delta before it is treated and dumped into the Fraser River. On hot humid summer days, this is unavoidable knowledge and not something to brag about. In 1988, North Delta hit the big screen, when Jodie Foster came to town and filmed the controversial gang rape scene in *The Accused* at the infamous sketchy dive bar on River Road. These were the things we knew about our home.

We also knew that on Friday nights, Scott Road would transform from being a thoroughfare to being a cruising strip. Pickup trucks and loud music — rock, metal and eventually bhangra — crowded the long strip and pockets of young people hovered in 7-11 parking lots, McDonald's parking lots and any other unused lot. This was before they'd make their way to the Bog to do whatever it was they did while people like me stayed home. Hiding. Hiding was what you did when the world seemed full of predators. Friday nights for me, and for my friends Lynde and Elaine, most likely meant a trip to Safeway, a McCain Deep 'N' Delicious cake, a litre of milk and a board game, or TV, or a video.

Then, on Mondays, we'd hear about what we had missed (or successfully avoided): a fistfight here, a drunken barfing there, a possible pregnancy.

If we had been intellectual snobs, too smart or too goody-goody to take part in Friday night culture, that would have been one thing. I wasn't a nerd, because I didn't make the cut: I had neither the grades nor the discipline nor the ambition. What Lynde and Elaine and I had instead was a common belief that everything sucked.

By the time I was in high school, I thought it might be wise to take up some extracurricular activities to divert my parents' and teachers' attention from my bad grades. I had given up on institutional learning and so I had taken it upon myself to become home-schooled. Unfortunately for me, home-schooling requires not just parental consent but all kinds of paperwork which I did not have. I only got the home part right; I simply didn't go to school. I preferred the library or the Tim Horton's on Scott Road or Michael's Pizzeria in the strip mall next to Lumberland. Since I'd been absent for almost half of my Grade 12 year, and I wasn't particularly bookish to begin with, my report cards were not indicative of the great strides I was sure I was making.

My strategy was a good one. I would distract all the concerned adults, particularly those who had put forth theories that I was depressed or anti-social, with my impressive list of interests. I have never been good at sports so I didn't join any teams. I couldn't be involved in the yearbook because it meant staying after school, which would have achieved the opposite effect of what I wanted. I wasn't interested in book clubs or music lessons or interpretive dance. My two friends, Elaine and Lynde, despised extracurricular activities and the very idea of them. Because we had a perverse sense of irony, Lynde and I joined the North Delta Pride Committee. The club met on the last Wednesday of every month at a different member's home for cookies and juice and a discussion about what could be done to improve the spirit of our community.

For the most part, the purpose of the North Delta Pride Committee was to foster a sense of kinship. In practice this meant that the prominent members were realtors who were busy passing out their contact cards and homemakers who felt a need to connect with their neighbours to discuss issues like block parenting and the annual parade through Annieville, the historical section of "old" North Delta. There was also the token police officer who confessed to Lynde and me that he had put in an appearance as part of the Delta police force's efforts to connect with the community.

Lynde and I were fascinated by these people. We were judgmental of them and figured their lives must be horrid and empty but, like scientists studying caged mice, we couldn't stay away. We went to all of the North Delta Pride Committee meetings and, though we sat at the back and said nothing, were thought of as two good kids with a keen sense of responsibility and maturity. The committee became fodder not just for our gossip ("Can you believe they can care so much about a stupid welcome sign?") but it solidified our theory that North Delta was the worst place on earth, a place so boring, so mundane that its victims could not even fathom their own imprisonment. In our own interpretations, we were living out *Twilight Zone* nightmares, counting the days until we could graduate and *get the rock out of Dodge* (whatever that meant).

When worries arose (via either teachers or parents) that I might be depressed, all I had to do was defer to my North Delta Pride Committee cohorts, Dolores-the-homemaker and Brent-the-realtor, who vouched not only for my attendance but for my enthusiasm. Lynde and I had figured out how to beat the system; we were proud indeed.

Since North Delta was, for the most part, developed in the late sixties with its first permanent population boom in the early seventies, it seemed that no one was really from there. Of course, we didn't know back then about the ancient village site next to the Bog. The area now known as North Delta is one of very few continuously occupied human settlements in North America. Archaeologists estimate that people settled on the land roughly nine thousand years ago. But to a suburban teenager's eyes, the sixties was when it all began.

Lynde, Elaine, and I bonded around being from very far away. Lynde's mother grew up in Texas and so she had the maverick

appeal of being a genuine cowboy-woman. Elaine was actually born in North Delta. Her parents had come from Canton, and the Yongs ran a diner on Scott Road where Elaine worked most afternoons. She also took Cantonese classes on Sundays and could kill spiders — or any insect, really — with her bare hands. Since I was from Denmark, there was no need for any of us to take on the psychological ramifications of the turf. We didn't need to succumb to the stigma.

Elaine could take her language skills and her practical business sense anywhere. She was the glamour girl of the bunch, the best behaved, the best dressed and the most likely to succeed. Lynde would point out that I could just as easily be wandering through the streets of Copenhagen, stepping into an old café to read Hans Christian Andersen, sipping a cappuccino and eating a pastry, instead of being in North Delta, walking to Michael's Pizzeria, where cheese bread was two dollars and coffee was only twenty-five cents.

And, in turn, Elaine and I would point out that Lynde could have spent her morning bronco busting, maybe breaking in her

This was the sixties, North Delta-style: mud, concrete foundations, stacks of two-by-fours, and modern suburban houses for young families. DELTA ARCHIVES 2004-3-68

new boots. Or she could have been out shooting at bottles for tar-
get practice and telling strangers to get off her land.

That was the beauty of knowing we were from someplace else.
We could imagine those places however we wanted and no one
could tell us we were wrong. Just because we happened to be
stuck in the boonies right now didn't mean we had to be there
forever. Besides, unlike most North Delta kids, we could blame
our parents. We were absolutely positive that our lives would have
been better if it hadn't been for our parents' silly (and, frankly,
selfish) decisions to move to North Delta. Ours was a simple reality, one that did not reflect all of the complexities involved in our
parents' decision-making processes. They had chosen to plant us
in this hell hole where we didn't get along with our peers, where
we were treated as outsiders and mocked for being different. Now,
here we were, wandering up and down Scott Road, aimlessly and

Kennedy endlessly searching for coolness. For a couple of months, a cof-
Heights fee shop opened in the Kennedy Heights strip mall. The owner
Dance Hall was a big hairy man who made a good cappuccino so Elaine and
on Scott Lynde and I scraped together our respective three dollars a couple
Road, 2009. of times per week for our big splurges at Euro Café. Other than
MARK MUSHET the Euro, the closest decent cappuccino was in New Westminster,
PHOTO which was a twenty-minute bus ride and then another ten minutes

away by SkyTrain. Why it mattered so much that we drink cappuccinos and not regular coffee was a simple matter of snobbery. We liked the aesthetics of the tall clear glasses, the way the hairy man would create three distinct layers between the espresso, the milk and the foam. As a term of endearment, Elaine dubbed him The Beast and it began to feel as though he was one of us, even though we never told him that. He was skilled and if it weren't for the fluorescent lighting and the Kentucky Fried Chicken next door, you could almost fool yourself into believing that this coffee shop was someplace else.

The question of why my parents moved to North Delta haunted me for many years, even after I moved away from there, which I did at eighteen. Naturally, the easiest way to understand their motivations would be to ask them. I tried. That approach was unsatisfying. Their story, like most immigrant stories, has morphed many times. Each upgrade — their divorce, my dad's subsequent moves to South Africa, Hong Kong, Brazil, and Seattle, my mom's post-secondary education and her self-employment — signifies a new version of the story. No matter what their answers reflect now, it's a retrospective version, just as mine is, a glossing-over of many small details: the details that go into deciding whether to live here or there.

North Delta was a trap — a black hole, a representation of a life that I didn't want. The North Delta dream — as I saw it then — involved procuring a man, getting a mundane job and having children, without considering other ways of living. If I stayed in North Delta, I'd better get used to buying loaves of Wonder Bread at the Real Canadian Superstore and getting excited about the weekly drink specials at the Delta Lion Pub in Nor-Del (which is, of course, shorthand for North Delta).

When I left North Delta, three weeks after graduating from high school, I swore never to return. It was one of those brilliant teenaged moments of determination — the kind of resolute decision-making that I haven't been able to emulate since. It was based entirely in emotion and involved no regard for the practical reality that my mom continued to live there, and in fact still lives there. It's fabulous to experience such resolve, even when it doesn't work out and you find yourself on a bus headed for Thanksgiving dinner only a few months after the resolution was made. Even after I was safely living in Burnaby (a place some people would still call "the boonies" but had tall buildings and was different), I got stomach aches every time I crossed the Alex Fraser. I felt like I couldn't breathe until I was safely back across the bridge in either New Westminster or Richmond heading towards Burnaby or Vancouver. It was very dramatic, not just because I was a teen or because I had been an outsider but because North Delta represented something to me — something awful that I needed to get away from.

I did get away. I went back to Denmark, to my mom's sister's home in a small Danish town where I could explore the answers to questions I couldn't help but ask: did I belong there? Was I more Danish than Canadian?

As it turned out, Denmark — for me, at that time — offered similar limitations, an indication that it was unwise to blame surroundings. Almost as soon as I set foot on Danish soil, I had residency status and a job interview.

I was hired at a horrible little kitchen gadget store where we listened to infomercials all day. I had one television behind me that played a 22-minute loop about an ecologically sound mousetrap; I had it memorized after the first day. There was another television just a few feet away that featured a stackable set of lunch boxes. This was a chain store and I'd gotten the job because I qualified for a Danish government program that placed youth in various jobs. This was where I met Thomas who explained the pun: the program we were both part of was called "Ung i Arbejde" which translates loosely to something like "Youth to Work" but in Danish sounds a little more like how we experienced it: "Dum i Arbejde" which translates much as it sounds, "Dummies to Work." The people we worked with were real idiots, we were convinced. Once Thomas and I recognized the solidarity between us, we talked about things like the inevitability of human extinction. We did this quietly so that our manager wouldn't hear and force us to do a new display window featuring mousetraps and jam jars.

Thomas, like me, carried an enormous amount of disdain for humanity that stemmed (as all cynicism seems to) from a level of disappointment he had not been prepared for. In his seventeen-year-old's wisdom, he was convinced that people were idiots capable of believing anything and he set out to prove it by starting his own fake cult. The prank consisted of creating a brand — a

Grecian pillar on which a human brain was perched — as well as a clever logo — "Tænk dig glad" or "Think yourself happy." He advertised meetings for the group — but he'd poster the meetings the day after. He even wrote letters to editors from the point of view of parents whose kids had been abducted into this cult.

Frustration coupled with action: that's what endeared me to him. There are plenty of people who feel impatient with the apathy they see around them. Very few start fake cults just to see if they can arouse some kind of response in the walking dead.

Before Thomas, it had been a lonely time of wandering through the cold windy cobblestone streets, glancing through shop windows at things I couldn't afford. Thomas grew up in that town, which, in its own way, was also the boonies. Even after I'd been there for six months, he was my only friend. He'd never been comfortable there; sticking out against the backdrop of homogenously blonde, blue-eyed small-town folk probably didn't help. No matter how stellar his adoptive parents, no matter how flawless his Danish, he was ethnically Korean and his black hair and tan skin provoked questions around his heritage that he was resentful of answering every time he met someone new. He left almost immediately after I did.

When I came back from Denmark, I parlayed my retail experience at the kitchen store into a job as a grill cook and found an apartment in Burnaby. Whenever I visited my mom in North Delta, I told myself that what I felt was nothing but my own discomfort. I was obviously projecting deeper "psychological issues" onto a neutral landscape and I should learn to knock it off. My disdain for North Delta stemmed from some kind of lack within myself.

Once in North Delta, I'd have flashbacks. Suddenly, I'd be back in remedial math class, with the other students all chanting "smoke break, smoke break" in unison, feeling the smallness of my world and the shortness of my breath. If I'd been a smoker, I might have been able to take part in the solidarity factor but since I was the kind of student who was considered to be depressed (and not in that cool *Breakfast Club* way), I stayed out of the smoke break campaigning.

Or I'd spot someone from my graduating class. They'd be making a sandwich at Subway or pumping gas at the Esso station or working the checkout stand at Lumberland and I'd feel claustrophobic. This sounds horribly insulting and judgmental — which it is — but I felt trapped. I'd think: That could be me, or that would have been me if I hadn't run like mad or if I hadn't known Elaine and Lynde. I had spent my high school years the way I imagine a bear spends time in a leg-hold trap, wondering if there was anything I could do, any part of myself that I could gnaw off and sacrifice in order to escape.

Though we all felt the desperation, Elaine was sensible about it. She knew she would go to university and work really hard and make the kind of better life that her parents imagined for her. Lynde and I were dreamers in a practical landscape, hippies in a working class setting, artists swaying in the branches while our fellow citizens toiled the land — or worked at Delta Shoppers Mall. We weren't divas about it; we both worked, Lynde at a tortilla chip factory and I as a telemarketer and at the cafeteria at Kwantlen College in Surrey. Like Elaine, Lynde also had plans though hers involved a different kind of escapism — she wanted to build a cabin in the woods or hike the West Coast Trail and learn to start fires without matches and spear hares and escape capitalism. She wanted full scholarships to prestigious engineering programs at Ivy League universities. My friends were going places: they had dreams and they seemed to know on some intuitive level that all things come to pass, that this predicament we were in would change and that it wasn't always all bad, and one day we might actually feel differently about it.

Of course, we only spoke about how unhappy we were, how deeply depressing this place was and how remarkable it would be if we got out alive. "This place" — the other way of describing home — demanded conformity. It was strangulating and stifling for anyone determined not to follow suit. North Delta is the kind of place that has a lot of potential for those who belong. For people who liked having yards and cars and patio furniture and plastic basketball hoops in their driveways and affordable mortgages and access to amenities, it was a perfectly legitimate community. For us, it was hell.

If you were raised without religion, as I was, the concept of hell is abstract, a figure of speech. My concept of hell had nothing to do with eternal damnation but was, instead, this endless maze I found myself in. If you could figure a way out of the labyrinth, the puzzle would be solved and this hell or non-hell would either go away or stay behind. Lynde, Elaine and I didn't know what we would get up to but we knew that we would leave eventually and that, in the meantime, we had bus passes.

Cannery Days

Long before there were buses in North Delta, before there were even roads, there was a booming business on the North Delta riverbanks. This is the southern tip of the Fraser River, where it meets the ocean, 1,375 kilometres from its headwaters at Mount Robson in the Rocky Mountains. This idyllic spot was old news

A cannery in 1883. Abundant salmon is what first attracted Europeans to the Fraser Delta.
DELTA ARCHIVES 1970–1–403

Back in the day, the odd black bear could still be found in Burns Bog. Early North Delta resident Raynie Maxwell shot this one in the 1930s. DELTA ARCHIVES 2009-40-29

to Aboriginal folks whose legends tell the river's story from count-less perspectives, but for the Europeans and Americans who initially only passed through the area following their desires for gold, the Fraser River's salmon supply must have felt something like stumbling upon a horn of plenty. The search for gold brought thousands of men from Europe and America to the Fraser Valley. Women came, too, but aren't mentioned much in the newspapers or archives. The problem for most of these men was that by the time they made it here, the land had been staked, the gold had been found, and it was all too late. Many of them couldn't turn back empty-handed — it simply wasn't an option: they only had enough money to get here and assumed that they would strike it rich once they arrived. Since they were strong enough to make it here and too poor to leave, many of the would-be millionaires became part of the work force that developed British Columbia.

In 1870, Alexander Loggie opened the first successful cannery in the Fraser River delta, supplying British demand for canned salmon. Sockeye salmon was a favourite of British palettes and, as such, became a good profitable business in North Delta. In the boom period of North Delta's canneries, there were thirteen of them and they all functioned similarly.

There are few photos of the canneries. The ones that were taken make it clear that the canneries looked like tent cities, similar to the kinds of temporary dwellings that took shape all along the riverbanks all the way up to the Yukon and Alaska. Some burlap and some rope created just enough shelter from the rain to make sleep possible. There was no heat, no comfort, no security. In those days, there were two phone lines out, both were in Ladner and they reached as far as New Westminster. In other words, if you worked in a North Delta cannery, you were really stuck. North Delta's population used to double during canning season. Two thousand people came from June to September — the way folks now might go tree planting — to do back-breaking labour and sock away a few pennies for winter. Each cannery usually had a factory building manager's office and quarters, a cookhouse, a mess house, a general store and bunkhouses. Chinese camps and Native camps were separate. Some Aboriginal folks brought the whole village for the season, because it was short — only a few months — and families could stay together. Race and gender determined the kind of job one might get. Chinese men butchered and canned the salmon, Aboriginal women performed the cleaning and filling processes and white men supervised. A cannery operating to its full potential produced a thousand cans daily and required a work force of 150 people.

From the 1870s to 1880s, cans were handmade and hand-filled. They were manually soldered, then cooked, then pierced with an awl, vented, then resealed and cooked again. But it didn't take long before the procedures were entirely automated. Gang knives, solder baths and steam retorts were the latest technology and before long labelling machines were added too.

Cannery owners needed a workforce that was readily available but for the labourer, work was never guaranteed. Actual fishing was done only by men. In order to prevent overfishing, the Fisheries Act of 1875 limited the number of fishing licenses on the Lower Fraser to 500. The majority of these licenses went to cannery owners who hired European, Aboriginal and Japanese fishers. Individual fishers were forced to use the boats and licenses of the canneries that hired and exploited them. Two men shared a boat and shifts were often 24 hours. Individuals who worked for themselves could make 20 cents per fish. If you worked for a cannery, you'd make 10 cents a fish. Anyone who complained was promptly dismissed. The Fraser River Fisherman's Protective Association was established in 1893. By 1899, the Fisherman's Union emerged. The union was dominated by white male labourers who blamed Japanese labourers (rather than the canneries' monopoly) for their poor wages.

The Sto:lo, which means "the People of the River," often spent summers in the area now known as Burns Bog as well as the area where the canneries were. Several other First Nations including the Katzie and the Tsawwassen also used to spend summers in the area now known as Burns Bog.

Sto:lo territory actually stretches much further up into the area now referred to as the Fraser Valley, all the way up through Hope and Yale. Their oral history includes stories about being able to walk on the backs of salmon across the river during fishing season. These days, when newspapers are reporting that soon there won't be any salmon left at all in the Fraser, this kind of story seems like pure mythology. Imagine salmon populations so plentiful that you could walk on the backs of them to cross the river. Then imagine being in a work camp, catching, cooking and canning them.

Your Land, My Land

When I was in elementary school, we learned a song called "This Land is Your Land, This Land is My Land." We were taught the Canadian version but it is actually an American song. When Woody Guthrie wrote the song in 1940, one imagines he did it out of love. One imagines he was trying to foster a sense of inclusivity. It's a catchy song. I liked it. Some say that Guthrie wrote the song as a satire but I grew up singing it earnestly. I grew up to accept a paradigm of land ownership without questioning it. This song, along with "O Canada" and many others, normalized the very concept of land ownership on this continent for generations before me. The favourite playground phrase "go back to where you came from," uttered in my direction countless times, is just a rephrasing: this is not your land, this is my land.

The only way to wrap your mind around North America's history in a way that's even remotely sympathetic to our colonizing predecessors is to think that these early settlers, these migrants,

saw nothing but plentiful abundance and room enough for all. Blind to the concepts that land is borrowed, that humans are part of an intricate ecosystem, we are now seeing the repercussions of those early days.

The trouble, it seems, began with pre-emption, a concept that is nearly unimaginable today. The idea was that every man (yes, just men, and just white ones at that) was entitled to 160 acres of land for free if he was willing to develop it. This is the foundation of British Columbia's land tenure system.

North Delta wouldn't be North Delta if Ladner weren't Ladner. The Ladner brothers were Cornish and went to California in search of their fortunes. They had a mule carting business and then they caught wind of British Columbia's gold rush and turned their sights north. Like thousands of other men who left their southern and eastern lives in search of gold, the Ladner brothers faced the same harsh fact that most of the gold was gone by then — stakes had been claimed and for most folks that meant that the laborious search for gold amounted to toiling on someone else's land. This was not the vision they had. They were intent on creating a future, on making money and starting families. One of them must have noticed that the marshy lands they had to travel through at the mouth of the Fraser River were unclaimed and appeared to be the kind of land that would make ideal farmland.

Looking north across the South Arm of the Fraser River towards Richmond. In the years after World War II, most of the Fraser delta was still farmland. It was only in the 1950s that the area caught the eye of real estate developers. DELTA ARCHIVES 1970–1–21

It was rich and plentiful and even though they would have to find a way to drain the excess moisture, it was perfectly situated. They applied to the Crown (the English one, of course) and took what they could. Then they both took wives which allowed them to take more land. Then they both had children which allowed them to take even more land. Eventually, they had a whole lot of land and they were good developers with a keen vision. Ladner was drained ditch by ditch, many of which the Ladner brothers dug themselves. Eventually, they, along with the men they subcontracted to, built a structure known as the Ladner dykes. They still encircle Ladner's farmland, protecting them from the river.

They ended up with a different kind of gold mine: premium farmland. Both became active in their communities. Both cared about politics. Both were good businessmen. The Ladner brothers cashed in. Within a year, they had cultivated a good portion of their land and turned it around for profit. Within a decade, they had sold off an even larger portion of the land and created a town called Ladner, complete with its own port, Ladner's Landing, right at the mouth of the Fraser River, so that all of the gold rush travellers, the trades folk and the bride ships had a place to stop for supplies, food and rest. The Ladner brothers were astute at buying low and selling high and, in their case, this was extra profitable since "low" essentially meant free.

By proxy, the land that would later be known as North Delta became intriguing property. If these brothers could turn around their almost-free land for an enormous profit in a decade, then surely surrounding lands could yield good profit as well.

The Fire

These days, I'm pretty vocal about the importance of conserving Burns Bog but when I was a North Delta teen, I didn't get it. It wasn't until years after I moved away that I read in the *Globe & Mail* that the federal government had purchased 8,000 acres of the bog. I began to understand what North Delta was legitimately famous for, the Burns Bog, some 10,000 acres of raised spongy peat-covered land. It's not that I was unfamiliar with the Bog. It was in our local paper, *The Leader*, all the time. We heard about it when in the early 1990s, developers wanted to turn it into our

own version of the fabled West Edmonton Mall. We heard about the realtors wanting to develop condos for more commuters. Disney had dibs on it for a while and the kids at my school were all very excited about the idea of Mickey and Donald and all of those rides being so close to home. There was also some talk about it turning into a rodeo or a racetrack, just like the racetrack on Hastings Street in Vancouver (which, incidentally, was also built on a peat bog). Once it was supposed to be turned into the centre for a global communications network. When I was growing up, Burns Bog was thought of as a piece of undeveloped land, similar to all of the empty lots along Scott Road. Had I known better, I'd have spent my teen-angst energy helping Eliza Olson and the Burns Bog Conservation Society; but I was much more interested in destruction back then.

The Great Fire of 2005. The plume of smoke from Burns Bog could be seen as far away as Squamish.
ROB WEST
PHOTO

By the time I was in my teens, I'd have been happy to see the bulldozers attack the land. Even as an adult, watching the news about the fire in Burns Bog, I was hesitant to think of it as a nature reserve. To call it "the lungs of the Lower Mainland" seemed a bit dramatic.

The TV news on September 12, 2005 showed footage of 170 hectares of Burns Bog engulfed in flames. Interviews with distraught North Delta residents created fantastic television. Scientists were calling it a catastrophic emergency. I felt that I owed my home an emotional response. Anything else seemed insensitive.

I was in Squamish at the time and although I stayed politely by the evening news, I felt like I should have had a stronger reaction. I had been addicted to CNN when disaster struck New Orleans, New York, Thailand, any of the mythic places I'd wanted to visit.

The newscaster went on and on about how environmentalists would interpret the fire, what impact this tragedy might have on all of us. How Burns Bog is the largest raised peat bog in an urban area. How Burns Bog is the lungs of the Lower Mainland. How it might have been prevented. Watching my old stomping ground engulfed in flames, I was numb.

The next morning, having almost forgotten about the evening news, I went to the Sunflower Bakery to pick up fresh bread.

A cloud of thick dark grey smoke hung over Cleveland Street, the main stretch of Squamish. Ash covered my car. I couldn't believe it. Burns Bog was 100 kilometres away. Everyone at the Sunflower was talking about North Delta and the poor people who lived there.

As it turned out, the fire was actually good for the bog. Fires generally are. Trees are bad for bogs. Fires kill (or at least hinder) trees and are therefore good. First Nations people used to purposely set fire to the bog for this very reason. The cranberry yield the following season would be significantly better.

After the cattle ranch failed, Burns tried sheep. This photo of the Burns Ranch was taken during the 1920s. DELTA ARCHIVES 1988-39-03

Sheep on the Burns Ranch, Ladner.

Nº 15

Fire makes good television. For the first time in my life I was from the place that everyone was talking about, the place that was all over the news. It felt hollow and I felt phoney.

Patrick Burns, after whom the bog was named, was an ambitious tycoon who bought the land in the 1910s with the hopes of raising cattle there. Burns was from Oshawa, Ontario. He'd come west in search of cheap land on which to raise cattle for his great vision of running a meat packing company. At that time, Ladner was already booming as far as the farming industry was concerned. Ladner supplied most of the Lower Mainland with dairy and the land prices had skyrocketed because of it. Unfortunately for Burns, the area he bought — at an unheard-of cheap price — was mostly wetlands and useless when it came to raising cattle. Ladner had been wetlands, too, but the land had been dyked and drained. There were a few areas further up in North Delta, closer to what is now called Scott Road, that could be farmland, but even that land, because of its proximity to the bog (and by extension the peat), produced the kind of cattle that could not yield much value on the market. The dairy cows' milk could not make the cut due to sediments, and the enterprise was, all in all, a bust for Burns. Bogs are low in nutrients and in order to execute his cattle farm plan, he was literally forced to move on to greener pastures.

Burns was reputedly disappointed by the uselessness of the land — unlike Ladner, its neighbour to the south, Burns Bog and its surrounding area is not farmland — but Burns kept it because with the low real-estate value, it was more of a hassle to get rid of it.

Things turned out well for Burns in the end. Instead of a cattle farm on bog land, he built a warehouse on West Hastings Street in Vancouver. Eventually, he moved to Alberta where he gained distinction as one of the province's most rich and famous. On his 75th birthday, he was honoured with a cake that was at that time said to be the largest birthday cake in the history of the world.

Still, Burns Bog wasn't a complete bust as agricultural land. From the 1920s until the 1980s, Burns Bog peat was commercially harvested. Many who grew up in the Lower Mainland remember the refrigerator-sized plastic-wrapped bales of peat moss sold at garden stores. Burns Bog fertilized fields and gardens throughout North America.

Since the Ladner brothers settled in what is now known as the

Peat extraction, 1950s. For decades, Burns Bog peat fertilized suburban gardens throughout North America.
DELTA
ARCHIVES
2007–44–1

Corporation of Delta 150 years ago, thousands of hectares of vital wetlands have been destroyed. Wetlands are among the most threatened of Canada's ecosystems and, indeed, the northern hemisphere. They act as freshwater purifiers, flood controllers, and carbon sinks.

The bogs of the Lower Mainland have almost all been drained, dyked, and filled for agriculture and urban development. That Burns could not get his cattle farm up and running a century ago has proven to be a bounty just as many of the successful farms in the Fraser Valley are to our detriment. In the Fraser Valley alone, there are some five hundred kilometres of dykes protecting the commercial, agricultural, industrial and urban areas behind them.

Most wetlands are destroyed because of their proximity to urban centres. The problem with Vancouver's increasing popularity as a place to live — as well as a tourist destination, Olympic host and trade hub — is that the dollar value of the land surrounding Vancouver has increased dramatically over the past few decades. Even in times of supposed economic recession, the Lower Mainland is rapidly expanding. The phenomenon known as "urban sprawl" is, in fact, so prevalent that it has become mundane. These days, developers are bypassing the suburbs and creating "exurbs" in areas even further away from the metropolitan centres that were once critical to the desirability of real estate. Drive into the Fraser Valley and you will see smatterings of high-density condo "urban style" living in places nowhere near urbanity. These new neighbourhoods are simulacra, formed around parking lots of big box stores, banks, and trendy chain restaurants that offer the illusion of a destination point.

Bogs are crucial to the sustainability of life on this planet. They reduce the emission of greenhouse gases into the atmosphere. They provide biologically diverse habitats for rare species. Maintaining ecological balances within the bog environment is crucial. Bogs can provide critical information about cultural history. Though no "bog people" were ever found in Burns Bog, the nature of bogs is to preserve their own layers and, in so doing, they are an invaluable tool for tracing our past. Because of the high peat content and acidity, things don't decompose quickly in bogs. They are our museums, our encyclopedias and our connection to our collective history.

When the Alex Fraser Bridge was built in 1986, it split Burns Bog by running right through it. There was no consideration for what this might mean. It had the effect of eradicating black bears from the bog. When I was growing up, we heard about these things — mountain lions and bears walking through suburban streets, eating people's garbage. The bridge created a dividing line within the bog and it also divided North Delta, putting the bog on one side of the bridge and the suburban homes on the other.

Burns Bog, about five times the size of Stanley Park, is not park land. It wasn't until 2004 that it became federally owned. The Burns Bog Conservation Society and environmental non-profit organizations everywhere sighed a breath of relief for just

Commercial peat extraction continued until the 1980s, when this photo was taken. Hard to imagine this burning, but at the end of a dry summer, brush and small trees growing atop the bog are vulnerable to fire. DELTA ARCHIVES 2004-3-346

a moment but they didn't consider it a victory. Eliza Olson could tell you that just because land is officially "conserved" does not mean that it is safe or that the battle has been won.

When the South Fraser Perimeter Road is completed in 2012, Burns Bog will find itself surrounded on all sides by heavy traffic. While irksome to humans, the effect of such toxicity next to a piece of land that is already vulnerable will mean that many of the species that currently depend on Burns Bog for survival will die off.

I was so busy trying to get away from the landscape then that I didn't bother to look around. I didn't see that Burns Bog is one of the most beautiful places on earth. I didn't see the countless brave souls who gave their time, money and efforts to lobbying against its development. I didn't see those same people when they built boardwalks throughout the Delta Nature Reserve so that people like me could go for walks there without damaging the fragile ground beneath them.

Origin Stories

Most people feel a sense of conflict about where they're from. I have met people who say that they don't — people who were never at odds with their environments or parents or school or peers. Good for them. When I meet these people, I try not to let the conversation turn to where I'm from. Conflict of place is not something I'm good at explaining; people get it or they don't. Talking about my own conflicts to the conflict-free is frustrating and unsatisfying.

Like many Canadians, I come from several distinct places. There's the place I grew up, which is North Delta. I lived there from the age of six to eighteen. I lived in two different houses in two separate areas and went to three different schools. I knew every mall and street and fast food place. I knew the bus routes and held several jobs there.

Then there are the mythological places, which, in my case, do exist. These are the towns my parents are from. I have heard countless stories about these places and have been there several times, each time tracing my parents' steps, imagining my grandparents' homes and the homes of my great grandparents and their parents and their parents. These places are real and not-real simul-

taneously. One is a tiny fishing village on the west coast of Denmark and the other is a farm on Denmark's mainland, Jutland,
between the towns of Kolding and Fredericia. In both cases, I'm
speaking of the homes of my great-grandparents and their parents
and their parents. Even my grandparents' generation moved away
from those places of origin and by the time my parents were starting to settle down, they moved far away, leaving Denmark's mainland and buying a townhouse in a suburb thirty minutes outside
of Copenhagen. That place is Hoje Taastrup, where I was born.
According to my passport, this is where I'm from but I can only
remember nebulous details, like sitting on my dad's shoulders,
holding onto his head at a playground. I remember that our living *Kennedy*
room had olive-toned walls and a cream-coloured sofa with brown *Heights, a*
stripes. Or maybe I just think I remember this because I've seen *harbinger*
the evidence in photo albums. My grandparents and their parents *of the strip-*
and their parents would have found a move like the one my par- *mallification*
ents made, from small town to urban centre, unthinkable. *of North*

    And so it is with movement. *Delta, late*

    My·parents moved to Canada to start a new life and to afford *1970s. DELTA*
themselves more space and time and to give me the gift of fluent ARCHIVES
English and a culturally diverse environment. 2004-3-67

Before I left North Delta, whenever anyone asked where I was from, I'd say "Greater Vancouver." It was the truth but there was nothing "great" about it. Only persistent questioners could get me to say I was from North Delta. It was a fact I rarely admitted.

Now, when people ask me "Where's home?" I say "Vancouver." That's easy; I have a mailing address and a parking permit decal to prove it. There's a big difference between where home is and where you come from, though some people accuse me of being too complicated about the whole thing.

If you grow up loathing a place, resenting it as the backdrop for your life, is that home? What if, years later, you go back there and even though you hated it then, it seems worse now because they've torn down the remnant of the culture you knew to build big-box stores run by American conglomerates. You hated the strip malls but you'd rather have them than Taco Bell. Is that nostalgia?

All lives worth living have conflict and struggle and, early on, I decided to blame my alienation on my geographic location — which is not only alterable but ultimately circumstantial. I always had an idea that somewhere else there was a community that I belonged to, a place where I would feel happy and fulfilled. I searched for that community for a long time after I left North Delta. Only recently did I finally understand that I have brought North Delta with me. As the old adage goes (or *my* adage, anyway), you can take the girl out of North Delta but you can't take North Delta out of the girl.

Twenty-Four Million and Three

In 1981, my parents packed our lives into a container and sent it away. We took a ferry from Denmark to England and then a plane over the Atlantic and across Canada to the west coast. My dad found a job with a British shipping company in Vancouver and after a brief stint in North Vancouver, we settled in North Delta.

I was five and found the facts about our new home too abstract to follow. My dad tried to show me how Canada is 9,976,140 square kilometres whereas Denmark is 43,094. The family atlas was a big part of our father–daughter time. Denmark's population was 5 million whereas Canada had 24 million. Apparently, I asked things like whether that included our family. My dad, who has

always engaged my questions, held me on his knee and told me that that was our first order of business upon arrival in Canada — change the number. Once we got off the plane, Canada would have a population of 24 million and three.

North Delta's burgeoning neighbour- hoods were a magnet for young fami- lies in the 1960s and 1970s. DELTA ARCHIVES 2004-003-58

I am the same age now as my parents were when they made that journey. I can't imagine packing up my whole life into boxes, taking a chance on a job I might not like, and moving to a country where I barely speak the language. I don't have a child but I imagine it was a tough decision to relocate a kid who goes to school, has friends and friends' parents who babysit.

In Canada, a family could still get by on one income. A family of three could live, as we did, in a huge house with a wrap-around garden. Wilderness still engulfed cities. The pace of life was different. Canada fulfilled dreams; it was a less violent version of America.

At the final goodbyes, my aunts and uncles, grandmother and cousins all came to the ferry terminal to see us off. My cousin later recalled the sadness of the day, waving goodbye to us, the whole family thinking that they might not ever see us again and that, if they did, we would be different.

People in my family are partial to practical jokes. My uncles and cousins stayed up the night before and scoured the town for the biggest cardboard box they could find. They gift wrapped it and, just before takeoff, told my parents they had a final surprise. The oversized gift was supposed to be a comedic comment on the fact that my mom is an excellent planner. She does everything right. She is the kind of traveller who calls airlines to cross-reference the permissible mass-to-weight ratio of her luggage so she can bring the maximum. She knows exactly how much she is allowed to carry on board and she knows how much she is capable of carrying. This being such an important juncture, I can only imagine that she was even more prepared than usual. The joke failed. The uncles dragged in a gigantic fake gift box and my mom burst into tears. She had barely slept, she had no home, she had put everything on the line and now she was supposed to graciously accept a trinket the size of a giant refrigerator. That story is still the family's cautionary tale about practical jokes. Timing is everything.

Because I was only five at the time, I wasn't emotionally invested in the immigration process. I was more interested in spending time with my imaginary bee. It was my best friend, a possible result of being an only child or at the very least someone who needed to make up her own entertainment a lot. My parents humoured me with the fantasy and the bee became a part of the family, joining us at mealtimes and travelling with us wherever we went. Unfortunately, the bee, like my uncles, also had bad timing. Just as we were boarding the plane in England, the bee flew away. My mom recalls this moment as even more horrifying than the gag gift. Would she have to drop everything to chase after an imaginary bee and have an imaginary conversation so that this make-believe bee would come back and the universe would be restored to its natural order? My mom, my poor mom, was stressed to her limit.

I apparently shrugged and told her the bee would meet us on the other side. I know the mind plays tricks and that memory is fallible but I can still hear my mom laughing with relief.

Bogged Down

North Delta, with its population of just over 50,000, is similar to many Canadian suburbs. Nearly half of all Canadians live in low-density neighbourhoods outside of urban centres. Just like in America, we adopted a post-war suburban sprawl tactic, spreading ourselves out as we bought cars and washing machines, swing sets and houses. North Delta's story, while unique, is not exceptional; it's typical.

According to Statistics Canada, most recent immigrants choose to live in high-density urban centres, as do most university graduates. My parents didn't graduate from university and when they immigrated, they were clearly searching for a kind of "authentic" Canadian experience. My parents didn't want to live in East Vancouver where most of the other European immigrants lived. They didn't want to live in Burnaby close to the Danish Lutheran Church or in North Vancouver where the Danish butcher shop, Jolly Meats, sold all of the grocery items we couldn't buy in North Delta, at least not in the eighties.

We got the authentic experience. My friends and I knew we didn't live in the Big City. We knew we were different from the kids who did. North Delta is not far enough away from Vancouver to be its own place. Its identity is, in part, based on its proximity to Vancouver. Its relative distance from the Big City is key in its appeal or lack of appeal. Realtors like to boast about the quick commute, the access to big city amenities and culture. The whole concept of suburbia is based on this very idea of a quiet place to sleep. As theories go, this idea of living close to a busy metropolis is an interesting one. Anyone who has spent much time in suburbia knows that very few people put that theory into practice. Very few people work downtown and spend their weekends and evenings commuting back downtown to catch the latest movie or take part in the city's culture. Yet many are comforted by the knowledge that they could, if they feel like it, get into their cars and within an hour, have a "night out".

But North Delta has its own culture. There is a vast diversity of folks who have come from far and wide in search of affordable property in a relatively low-crime, quiet place. If not for this great search, my friends' parents would not have come to North Delta and we might not have met. Sure, we were outsiders but, really, in a place that wasn't densely populated until the seventies, what does that mean?

My friend Surjinder and I met in Grade 2. We had good reason

The original wave of family-run restaurants which fed North Delta's workers and their families have given way to homogenous franchise outlets. DAN BUSHNELL PHOTO

to form a coalition as we were the only two kids in our grade who brought weird lunches. By "weird" I mean no bologna sandwiches or Fruit Roll-Ups. We quickly learned to congregate at the far end of the playground where her roti and my pickled beets and liver paté would be safe. If there was one thing we were sure of it was that we would not be able to barter our lunches with the other kids. No amount of rye bread could yield a Wagon Wheel and that was that.

One year, my mom organized a birthday party for me. Perhaps this was an attempt to win the favour of the more mainstream North Delta children. Surjinder couldn't come because, according to the Nanakshahi calendar, my birthday falls on the birthday of Guru Hargobind and is a holy day. My mom did her best to organize a nice party for me but even at eleven, I hated making small talk. The girls from my class had petty preoccupations like boys and clothes, details that would catch my fleeting attention later but not at the time.

A couple of years later, I met Elaine. We were in Grade 8 and became friends when we consistently tied for last place in the one-kilometre runs around the Sungod Arena in gym class. We were ousted to outfield whenever any team sports were forced upon us. We were also in Foods and Nutrition together, a course in which we excelled and connected over our love of cinnamon quick breads. This situation, combined with our shared disdain for gymnastics, basketball, volleyball, softball and hockey was the only basis required for a friendship.

By the end of high school, her parents called me an honorary member of their family. What they meant was that I spent countless evenings watching television in their basement or lounging about on the velvet floral couch in their living room or eating their food. Like my parents, Elaine's had come to North Delta from far away. They were from Canton via Macau via Peru, though I didn't understand much about their past until years later. They ran Henry's Chinese–Canadian Restaurant on Scott Road. Elaine's parents, Henry and Cecile, escaped Chairman Mao's communist regime in China. They wanted no part of it. Cecile's dad had managed to get out on a travel permit and had moved to Peru and applied for citizenship and was able to help the young couple come over. Finding salvation in Peru, they settled there for some years until one day they found themselves in the middle of a revolution again. What could they do? They got married and travelled to Canada for their honeymoon, and a new start. They were only allowed to bring one thousand US dollars.

Neither of them spoke English. Cecile became pregnant and her son, Henry (named after his father, of course), was born in a Canadian hospital and was therefore a Canadian. Cecile and her husband Henry lived in a shared bedroom in a shared house in Strathcona with no heat. Cecile remembers begging the landlord to turn up the heat just a little bit because she was scared that her baby would get sick. She was only twenty-one at the time and had already moved around the world twice. They were ready for someplace calm and stable. Henry took a job packing poultry trucks in Chinatown until they saved up enough money to rent a diner to run. After searching for the right place, they found an affordable location on Scott Road in North Delta. They found a home a few blocks away and started renovating the restaurant. On their first day open, they made five dollars.

Big Sundaes, Big Dreams

Henry's Chinese–Canadian Restaurant is long gone, but the Dairy Queen is still there — even the back-splash tiling is unchanged since I went there with my grand-mother from Denmark.

DAN BUSHNELL
PHOTO

Everything in North Delta was big. A house the size my parents bought would have been unthinkable in Denmark. Around the corner from where we lived, at the Delta Shoppers Mall on Scott Road, you could buy giant vats of mayonnaise at the Extra Foods and queen-size panty hose at the K-Mart. These things were not only impressive but impossible to come by in Copenhagen, and a big part of the new world's exotic attraction. Part of impressing Danish relatives who came over to visit was exposing them to big things.

The summer I turned nine Delta's local paper, *The Leader*, carried a coupon advertising a special deal at the Dairy Queen on Scott Road: half off a banana split, three big dollops of soft-serve draped with chocolate, pineapple and strawberry sauces and sandwiched between a halved banana, covered in fake whipped cream and topped with a maraschino cherry. It was, naturally, the most coveted coupon of the summer. Hinting at following up on the ad's welcoming suggestion to "come on in" depended very much on what kind of mood my mother was in and who she had just

been talking to. There was some concern that I was developing what they called an American body type. The best strategy, I had learned, was to say nothing about the treat itself but to comment on the economic advantage of a coupon. This would show her that I'd been paying attention to her lessons on saving and smart spending. My mom cut the coupon out and thumbtacked it to our cork bulletin board, "for when your grandmother visits," she smiled, secretive.

In Canada, or at least in North Delta (which to me meant Canada at that time) banana splits and other cool treats were part of a normal summer. Back in Denmark, certainly in my family, that kind of sizeable dessert was simply unheard of. Danish kids would share a treat that size four ways.

When my dad's mother finally arrived from Denmark twenty-six days after the initial clipping of the ad, I was eager for her to unpack, change into her "outside" clothes and walk to the Dairy Queen with me. That she needed to adjust to the new time zone was, to me, a terrible inconvenience. I didn't understand until years later that our genetic material shares the same easy-going quality and if there's one thing we don't do in this family, it's rush. It makes us cranky. My grandmother, my father and I, we don't respond well to set schedules and enforced procedures. We need nap time and freedom to sit and think or to just sit. It also took me a long time to figure out that the family was divided on the issue of sitting and doing nothing. It bothered my mom.

In fact, by day three or four of my grandmother's visit, my mom resorted to suggesting the "grandmother–granddaughter" activities. While we went off to poke around at K-Mart or walk around the block or sit in the back yard playing rummy, my mom tore around like a herding dog gathering its flock, doing laundry, getting groceries and cooking meals, making it all seem effortless. The senior and junior matriarchs were preoccupied.

It was on one of these fun-filled afternoons that my grandmother and I, at last, walked to the Dairy Queen. She held my right hand and, in my left hand, I held the newsprint ad and a $5 bill that my mom had passed to me earlier that day, crisp and clean from her faded leather wallet.

I ordered a banana split at the counter while my grandmother stood, silent, beside me. She nodded with pride at my fluent English, an ironic compliment given that she couldn't speak the language.

We sat at the orange vinyl booth, my legs sticking to the bench, my grandmother politely dabbing at the perspiration on her forehead with a thin white handkerchief.

They called the banana split on the loudspeaker and I sprang up to fetch it. When I brought it back, my grandmother started shaking her head back and forth, "No, no, no." She seemed almost angry and protested that we couldn't possibly eat that creation.

I'd been waiting for weeks and was optimistic that we could. She clearly lacked confidence in our abilities. I took a bite. The sweet, cold soft-serve against the backdrop of the room-temperature banana, smothered in sauces, was so completely delectable that I barely noticed how little my grandmother ate.

Many mouthfuls in, I realized that she had been watching me all along. I didn't feel self-conscious eating around her. If anything, being around my grandmother brought out my hunger and my cravings. Her purse was always stocked with some kind of candy: salt liquorice, dark chocolate, wine gums.

If my mom had been in charge of her mother-in-law's purse, the motivational candies would have been distributed far less frequently. After all, it wasn't her side of the family that had the eating problem, it was my dad's. It was, by implication, my grandmother and me.

I remember how my grandmother used to walk slowly alongside me. She was the best sidewalk companion, as interested in tiny finds and looking for fallen coins as I was. Money that had been dropped by others was magic. I wasn't raised to think of God but on those miraculous days when I'd spot a quarter or crumply faded dollar bill tucked under a shrubbery, I could imagine for a moment that my life was blessed and that there was a deity who wanted for me to have the Big League Chew or the Pop Rocks that my mom cruelly denied me.

At the Dairy Queen, I noticed how carefully and slowly my grandmother ate. She wasn't a delicate woman, she had big hands and was solidly built and would not have called herself a beauty, though to me, she was the most gorgeous woman I'd ever known. This wasn't just a superficial judgment of her appearance, it was about her mannerisms and her presence. She wasn't much for smiling. Her face was stern, distant. She didn't talk to random strangers, not like my mom who had figured out that the real way to get along in a Canadian neighbourhood was to make conversations about the length of a lineup or how irritating it was that you had to put a quarter into a shopping cart to be able to use it. My grandmother did not share thoughts like that with other people.

She savoured each mouthful of the banana split, eating extraordinarily slowly and making "mmmm" noises each time her spoon dove into the melting mass. As we shared the big banana split, I'd catch her nodding to herself, like she was agreeing to something in a private conversation that did not concern me. We were very good at being quiet together.

When I go back to North Delta now, I still like to stop in at the Dairy Queen once in a while. Nothing there has changed. It reminds me of childhood, with the mustard floral tiles, the rickety freezer full of cakes and the neon orange booths.

It used to be that the Dairy Queen where my grandmother and I ate our banana split was the only place like it around. Dairy Queen seems to be the harbinger in suburbs like Delta, a sign of the changes to come. It slips in under the radar. No one questions cool treats. People like soft-serve. It's harmless. Delicious even. It's not the same as McDonald's or other fast food joints. It's not ugly like that. But inevitably, Dairy Queen paves the way for a certain type of progress.

Back then, Scott Road was still undeveloped lots with for-sale signs and a few stores and apartments scattered around. When I go back now, the Dairy Queen, with its retro storefront, is tucked in among all of its big brothers. Now, in North Delta, you can get any kind of fast food you want.

I started Grade 1 in North Delta in 1982. Bill Bennett, British Columbia's premier at the time and Bill Vander Zalm, his minister of education, had just slashed funding to a wide range of school programs and publicly blamed school teachers for not doing their jobs properly. Just as the word "liberal" has little to do with the political party, my mom was alarmed by the misleading nature of the label "Social Credit". As my mom bluntly puts it, I just had to make do without understanding the world around me. The same was true for her. This is true for every immigrant child and is especially strange when you've already learned how to talk and how to understand but nobody speaks your language. When you add to that that no one wears the kinds of clothes you do or eats the kind of food you eat, it's easy to see how immigrant kids find each other and form a kind of alliance.

Surjinder's dad had recently moved here from Bombay and her mom was still there waiting for the paperwork to go through. We also befriended Wendy, whose parents were Jehovah's Witnesses, which meant she had to stand out in the hall during the Lord's Prayer. She was also absolved from making Halloween and Christmas crafts, though she did have to sing "Auld Lang Syne" with us.

My mom learned English by reading the *Vancouver Sun* every morning. She also watched the news regularly. My dad had to speak English at work and so my parents made a rule — one for which I am grateful today — that we only spoke Danish at home. As my dad has later put it, this is where a lot of immigrants screw up — they let their kids show off their new English skills at home and pretty soon they've forgotten their own language and have no choice about where home is.

The Temple

Years after I moved away, I made friends with a hippie woman who was into yoga and spirituality. On the surface, she was a prim, pearl earring-wearing woman who always wore funky clothing and had fashionably coiffed hair and elegant mannerisms. At that time, around 2001, Vancouver was turning into the kind of landscape that supported women like her. Yet she was not like the others; she didn't wear stretch pants from Lululemon; she didn't greet people with "namaste." She worked six days per week and spent her free time volunteering at a Sikh temple in Vancouver. At the gurdwara, she'd stack chairs or do custodial service. She never said she liked doing these things; she told me she felt compelled. There was a depth about her, or perhaps it was sadness, something I couldn't quite figure out. She was, by anyone's definition, a beautiful woman who received plenty of attention from admirers yet she didn't indulge in what she considered "ego-driven" activities. She'd found a greater purpose, she would say, but it didn't seem to make her happy.

She used to tell me about her son who lived in Kamloops. She'd

talk about how their relationship was improving, how they had had a difficult period. She divulged that he hadn't quite turned out as she'd expected but that you have to love people for who they are, no matter what, especially family. She was very good at analyzing and discussing the philosophical and theoretical nature of love. She pointed out that the greatest love was to be found in motherhood but that even motherhood was fraught with ambivalence. You risk that your children don't turn out as you hope. She'd recall what a good boy her son had been and how happy he'd made her when he was little. She was vague about his shortcomings in adulthood and I had the impression that perhaps he'd become a banker or developer, or maybe he drank too much. She abstained from alcohol and was dutiful in her belief about the corruption that drinking could lead to, and mostly surrounded herself with folks in AA even though she had never been an alcoholic. She also didn't eat meat and didn't take time off for herself. If there was any pleasure to be had, chances are, she would abstain.

She grew up Catholic but had turned to Sikhism because the religion was more peace-loving than what she was used to. She liked the customs and rituals. She liked the idea of wearing a sari, the femininity of the fabric, the cheerful bright colours. She enjoyed the feeling of community that she found at Temple

Guru Nanak Singh Gurdwara on Scott Road. MARK MUSHET PHOTO

and was eager to spend her weekends there even though most of her service involved kitchen work or scrubbing floors. Though it smacked of cultural appropriation to my Liberal Arts ears (I was in Women's Studies at the time), she was earnest in her efforts and I admired her zeal. Like many urbanites who turn to divine wisdom, she exuded conflict.

She blamed herself a lot, harshly critical of her efforts as a single mother. She talked about how she wished she had spent more time with her son, and sometimes she'd tear up and tell me there was never enough time — that he grew up so fast while she was running around getting odd jobs and moonlighting to pay the rent.

A new generation of North Delta families are following in the path of my friend Elaine's folks, working long hours in family-run restaurants so their own children can have a better life.
MARK MUSHET
PHOTO

Then, one night, she told me that she needed to confess something she'd never told anyone. She made me swear never to tell
and I agreed. She told me that technically her son does live in
Kamloops but, more to the point, he's in prison there. She asked
me if I remembered the hate crime that happened out in Surrey in
1998 at the Guru Nanak Temple. I did.

To understand the significance of what happened, one would
have to be privy to the social climate, the escalating tensions in
North Delta and Surrey, and her son was, as he had moved to Surrey some years before. Sur-Del, the quaint name for an informal
area that straddles Surrey and Delta, and a stretch three blocks on
either side of Scott Road, is the official border between the two
cities. Sur-Del is home to a thriving Punjabi community, so much
so that many shop signs and even street signs have abandoned
English or make a merely perfunctory attempt at bilingualism.

When my family moved to Sur-Del, it was a predominantly
white neighbourhood and, as with many white neighbourhoods
that become increasingly diverse, there was a good deal of resis-
tance to change. Perhaps it didn't occur or matter to most of the
white families that they, too, had only been there for a couple of
decades. Whatever the reason, the rhetoric at the time was very
"us-and-them".

When the Kennedy family developed houses and strip malls in
North Delta in 1967, they weren't just creating a new domestic
landscape; they were making a statement — imposing a stylistic
ideal on a landscape that would resist it. This was the vision of
suburbia in the late sixties and it was not that different in California or Ontario or Virginia or Alberta. The idea of living a conve-
nient car ride away from one's workplace was predicated on a level
of post-war privilege. North Delta was not actually intended for
immigrants or the lower-income single-families that it currently
caters to. The Kennedies, it seems, saw North Delta as the next
West Vancouver — an idyllic spot, affluent, surrounded by natural beauty, just far enough away from the big city to create a kind
of oasis.

What actually happened was, of course, far more interesting.
North Delta became a destination point for many immigrants,
a place, like Chinatown had been many decades earlier, where
families could prosper outside of the dominant culture. North

Delta, along with South Delta and South Surrey, is now home to a thriving economy in its own right, one that does not require commuting to Vancouver. What actually happened therefore angered a good number of people with a different vision.

The first onslaught of anger that I remember clearly was when Malaysian-born Sur-Del resident Baltej Singh Dhillon, a member of the Royal Canadian Mounted Police, fought for his right to wear his turban while at work. I was eleven or so when this story started appearing in the headlines of our local paper. Much outrage was expressed over Dhillon's insistence on his right to wear his turban at work. For them, the RCMP uniform had a certain sanctity that a turban — worn for religious reasons — did not. People had an idea of what Canada was and what Canadians, by extension, should look like. Just as a lot of folks favoured our big mountains and big trees, they also favoured certain aesthetic qualities in the RCMP and it became apparent that Sikhism was not one of them. This was the kind of conversation that was alien to my family and the Yongs. It smacked Canadian purism and what did we know about that?

A wave of anti-Sikh feelings swept through Sur-Del. Some people even made a quick buck by producing a calendar of photos that could only be described as vicious and ignorant, rampant with depictions of the fate that could befall the RCMP if turbans tainted the precious uniform. Though I never saw one, 13,000 calendars were sold that year. There was clearly a market for this "contribution" to the debate. Over 150,000 signatures were collected in a public outcry against Dhillon. The debate seemed to pivot on the idea of a national symbol.

But wasn't Canada supposed to be multicultural? All through school, I remember teachers describing the very different metaphors for cultural diversity. America saw itself as a melting pot, an image that requires a level of assimilation. Canada, on the other hand, was supposed to be a multicultural mosaic, a place where it was okay to be from here and from other places, too. So the sentiments of "This Land is Your Land," which was problematic to begin with, was far from accurate about Canada, and especially so about my own backyard.

Much of this discussion was obscured by a debate about the difference between the representational value of a Stetson hat and a turban. Finally, in 1990, the federal Solicitor General, Pierre Cadieux, who was responsible for the RCMP, gave his ruling. "Today, I'm announcing the government's decision which is not only the correct one in law but also the right decision." Dhillon would be allowed to wear his turban.

One would imagine that the permission granted to wear sacred headgear — this great gain for human rights and ethnic diversity — would serve our communities well, but it is my impression that tensions in the Sur-Del area only escalated after Dhillon's victory. This was indeed a symbolic time and just as there was a triumphant side, there was also a side that felt they had lost something. Many on this side were folks I went to school with or their parents — people who had bought houses in North Delta and made their homes on the premise that they could surround themselves with similar folks.

When my friend mentioned the hate crime that her son was involved in, I knew exactly what event she was referring to. Though I didn't know her son personally — he had grown up in Vancouver and moved to Surrey as a teenager — I knew a number of guys like him: guys whose paths also were not easy, who had different expectations from life than the lot they were granted. I knew these guys well and yet I still felt the palpable combination of chill sweat and horror as I stood across from my friend and pieced together the headlines I remembered and the connection they had to her. Nirmal Singh Gill, a sixty-five year old diligent family man, an immigrant to the neighbourhood going about his business, patrolling the temple grounds in the wee hours of a Spring 1998 morning, was kicked to death by five white supremacists. My friend's son was one of them.

In the 1980s, pround Mountie Baltej Singh Dhillon's successful campaign to wear his turban on the job signaled a new era in Canadian society.

She didn't share his hatred but she would never be able to figure a way out of this labyrinth of guilt and self-recrimination. Since it happened, she has put in countless hours scouring floors and stacking chairs at the Sikh temple in Vancouver in an effort to repay an impossible karmic debt.

Apathy and Chaos

My parents didn't explain God to me until I was in Grade 3 or so, and couldn't understand church, temples and Sunday school. Wendy's family didn't go to church either but she had Sunday school and Sunday clothing, notably a pair of glossy black lacquer ballet slippers. Surjinder had holy days, which often involved taking time off school and wearing really great outfits. They both had songs that nobody else in our school knew, and all around me it felt like my friends were taking part in something that brought them closer to their parents. On Saturdays, my parents liked to run errands so that was what we did as a family — go to the liquor store, buy groceries at Extra Foods and, if we were really filled with gusto, we'd drive to the Danish butcher in North Vancouver. It felt like my family was missing something. Most weekends my parents slept in while I watched Saturday morning cartoons. Eventually my dad would fumble out of bed, go into the kitchen in his brown velvet robe and make scrambled eggs. My parents liked to stay up late and hang out in the living room, smoking, sharing wine and stories and often listening to a new record — Neil Young or Paul Simon or Abba or Zamfir, depending on what my dad had picked up at A&B Sound. The later they stayed up, the louder the music would become and the greater the odds were that they'd hit the stash of Danish chocolates my mom hid in the antique buffet in the dining room. I could almost always hear from my room this cupboard door open and, like a dog responding to a high frequency whistle, I'd get out of bed to heed the call.

On one of those nights, sitting in the living room, sprawled out on the green shag rug, I remember asking them about this God stuff. My dad was pretty low-key about the whole thing and my mom generally approached things from a practical angle. She told me that life is about being ethical and kind, that meaning comes down to behaviour. But I wanted to know about the guy on the clouds in the sky.

God, she eventually told me, was something like Santa Claus —
something other kids were encouraged to believe in, something
best not to talk to them about in detail. My parents figured I'd
make my own decisions once I was old enough. The explanation
was anti-climactic though it did confuse me that my mom sometimes went to the Danish church in Burnaby. She told me that was
different; that was about meeting other Danes.

By the time I was in Grade 10, I wanted to know more about God-
Santa. I sat next to a boy named Shahin (who, at the time, went by
Shawn) that year in Social Studies. When he took a day off for his
religion, I asked him about it and he told me that Baha'u'llah, the
prophet-founder of the Baha'i faith, was the most recent of many
messengers from God. He explained that they didn't see Muham-
mad or Jesus or Moses or Buddha as any less valid, that there was
actually only one true God and that this God communicated to
us via various prophets at various times according to our collective capabilities. He explained how we needed many messengers
because we — humanity in general — didn't listen or understand,
so God had to send the message in different ways and at different moments to reflect our maturation levels. This seemed reasonable. He also introduced me to a bunch of new people who
had exciting discussions that were so foreign to my reality that just
on that level, I felt as though I had come closer to understanding God-Santa. Instead of talking about brand-name clothing or
hair or dropping acid, these folks talked about things like destiny
and volition. It wasn't long before I was much more interested in
them than my peers at school — with the exceptions of Lynde and
Elaine, of course.

Shahin introduced me to other Baha'i families in North Delta
and Surrey. They invited me to their homes and they provided
snacks and reading material and slide shows and juice. This was
a new world, a brighter, more sophisticated world filled with
inquisition and wonder. By Grade 12, I was a regular at Don and
Fereshteh's monthly "firesides", evenings organized around an
idea or theme in which everyone was asked to contribute. Firesides are common among Baha'is as a gesture or invitation to pres-
ent and consider new points of view. Topics vary and, at Don and
Fereshteh's, the guest list was diverse and the discussion lively.
Naturally, I asked if I could invite Lynde and they welcomed us

both. Eventually, my mom started coming, too. Elaine was less interested in religion even though her parents had just converted from Buddhism to Christianity, a fact that I found curious but would later come to understand.

Though these evenings took place in yet another seventies-style boxy home that Lynde and I thought of as drab and dull, we somehow managed to leave our judgments behind. At a time when we were dismissed as depressed or idiotic or dramatic teenagers by almost everyone else, Don and Fereshteh asked us about our opinions. Not only did this feel good but it fostered long nights of walking through the empty streets, sometimes silent, sometimes lively, talking about whether everything was magical and meaningful or random and meaningless.

Like teenagers anywhere, my friends and I wondered what it all meant, and thought the Big City held the answers.

MARK MUSHET

PHOTO

Firesides were only one part of the quest. Lynde and I spent a lot of time hanging out at her house, eating microwaved Pizza Pops and listening to Bob Dylan. Her mom was an English teacher and their bookshelves were lined with Chaucer, Auden, Plath, Yeats, Ginsburg, Lorde and Donne. If we thought we had questions, all we had to do was look around to see the far greater, far more articulate askers of questions that surrounded us.

Having already read most of the poetry of the western canon, Lynde had become more interested in Taoism and quantum physics. I had not heard of either but she insisted that they had something to do with God-Santa as well. Lynde was a patient teacher. Since neither of us had anything better to do, we figured we would set out to answer life's big questions early on. This would mean no mid-life crises for us, we figured. Whenever we weren't hanging out in our mothers' kitchens, we went to the library.

The 312 bus was our vehicle to freedom. It went along 112th Street, conveniently close to school, all the way to 96th Avenue where it turned down the hill and pulled into Scott Road Station.

Along the way, the window seat revealed houses for sale, houses for rent, well-kept houses with hedges and empty lots. Most of North Delta had traded hands by the time I graduated but only decades earlier, during my bussing years, it was mostly undeveloped plots with "for sale" signs, owned by a small handful of families.

At the bottom of 96th Avenue, a road that had only been properly paved in time for Expo 86, there was a bump. At twelve, I started venturing out on my own and found it really fun that most Deltoids — at least most cool Deltoids — were into the bump. Maybe it's because we were riding our sugar highs from all the Chews and Lots-A-Fizz we could buy for our allowances. All the way down the hill, there'd be the anticipation. Who would do it? Would the bus driver be angry or would he join in? Either was possible. At the bottom, the bus would hit the bump and on a good day everyone on the bus would raise their arms up, like we were on a roller coaster ride, and scream and then laugh. I thought it was awesome.

But by the time Lynde and I started making our escapes to the Vancouver Public Library, the awesomeness had worn off. In spite of the Taoist teachings she read to me, neither of us was that interested in the journey; we just wanted to be at the final destination. Scott Road Station meant twenty-three minutes to Granville Station and another fifteen minutes to the Vancouver Public Library. Lynde was an accelerated student; I was struggling to pass. She was taking honours math; I was in remedial. She was on the Environment Club and in the Drafting Club, and she used to stay late to work on the school newspaper; I had no extracurricular activities. She was athletic; I hated sports. We weren't just an unlikely pairing; we were a challenge to the entire social fabric of the grading system. Had we not been forced to sit beside each other in French class, we never would have spoken. We were both bored, me because I had given up on the enterprise of learning French, she because she had just spent a year in France on an exchange and was sick of being held back by the non-fluent. Before long, we decided we were wasting our time sitting in school in North Delta, she because she was too smart and would ace her provincial exams anyway and me because I no longer cared about getting a diploma.

One day, she asked me to come with her to a lecture at UBC.

I can't remember what it was about — chemistry, physics, something with graphs and charts — but I remember feeling surprised and honoured that she thought I was actually capable of understanding it. I wasn't. I smiled and nodded my way through the lecture, thrilled that she had faith in my intellectual capabilities because I didn't.

In retrospect, I understand why Lynde's mom didn't care for our friendship, as it lead to skipping school nearly every other day and taking the bus as far away from North Delta as we could. Lynde's mom had expectations that I considered outrageous and unjust. She expected Lynde to get good grades, get into a good university and follow in her footsteps by getting a full scholarship. Lynde's mom had come from Texas to study at the University of British Columbia. That was where she met Lynde's dad, who was the son of one of North Delta's early landowners. Lynde's mom ended up in North Delta, married, then divorced, with two daughters, working as a high school teacher who was intent on catapulting Lynde and her younger sister into the best schools they could possibly get into. Even though I was Lynde's first real friend, I was a threat to the vision.

My quest for knowledge and answers (or even some kind of indication that there was greater purpose and meaning) was supported by one of the central beliefs of the Baha'i faith — that of independent investigation. The religion itself asserts that it is up to the individual to remain on a spiritual search, that pursuing spiritual goals takes a lifetime, that one must familiarize oneself with the holy texts of all major religions if one wants to tap into the divine knowledge that sages have built on since the beginning of time. This made sense to me but what really appealed was the notion of independence. The idea of being the agent in my own learning suited me perfectly, and I took the official teaching to mean everything from religion to science to poetry.

One day my Grade 12 English teacher, Mr. Burke, recited the Prologue to *The Canterbury Tales* — in Middle English — and I knew that I would not be able to feign apathy again. I wanted to recite things. I wanted to be well-read and well-rounded, to have seen the movies he referred to and to have read the books Lynde talked about. I set about becoming the kind of student I imagined Mr. Burke would respect.

Lynde and I took to writing notes — not forged notes from "Mom" but bold notes on our own behalf. They went something like this: "Dear Mr. Burke, we are seeking a real education and will therefore be unable to attend class this week as we will be at the library."

Once downtown, we were free. We could stop and hang out with the old men playing speed chess in front of the art gallery or buy a cup of coffee or dawdle if we felt like it. But we always ended up in the stacks at the old library, a building since turned into a gigantic music and video game shopping emporium.

It was at that site that I first encountered James Gleick, who profoundly changed everything, including my little life, by documenting the history of chaos theory in his book, *Chaos*. It was the first science book I ever liked, the only one I read on my own time and one of few that made me cry.

My love of chaos theory had something to do with the way I learned about it. Lynde and I spent most of our time at the library, reading and exploring the stacks with our special random approach to learning. We liked to pull stuff from the shelves. Sometimes, it would be some academic journal about changing trends in mechanical engineering but sometimes, we'd get lucky. I found the Satanic Bible just by pulling a book off the shelf in the religion section. Of course, I wondered if this was really a message from God-Santa.

After random reading, we'd wander over to the West End to a coffee shop that no longer exists. We might have had something to do with that by taking them up on their free refills. We'd each slap a dollar on the counter, and guiltlessly drink three or four mugs. Finally it would be time to catch that 312 bus back to North Delta. We had to finish up by 9 o'clock in order to walk back to the SkyTrain and get back to Scott Road Station in time to catch the last 312 at 10:30. Soon, the decision to be made was whether to catch that 312 back to North Delta at all.

Often, that last mug of coffee was the catalyst in deciding. We could hang out exactly where we were for a mere eight hours longer and catch the first 312 at 6 AM. We could then go home, shower, change and go to school, or not. Our coffee shop was open 24 hours so it was really up to us. The process was a simple one: call Lynde's mom and tell her Lynde was spending the night at my house, then call my mom and tell her I was spending the night at the Yongs'. By about 2 or 3 in the morning, when it was too late and too early to go home, we'd go for a walk around Stanley Park. One night, camped out on Second Beach, Lynde pulled a stick of incense from her backpack, lit it and planted it in the sand. The smoke made tiny curls in the air, separated and rejoined, patterning itself according to the wind while we read Yeats and ate granola bars.

Against the backdrop of the giant logs in the sand at English Bay, Lynde explained the intricacies of Gleick's book and told me that the smoke patterns created by the incense were measurable but unpredictable. I thought this was deep and profound. Lynde made me believe that if I could understand chaos theory, even though I barely passed Grade 10 science, then I, like the scientists that James Gleick wrote about, could be on the cutting edge. There was hope for me. I didn't find out until many years later that Einstein didn't get good grades and Stephen Hawking dawdled through his degrees until his illness forced him into the studious urgency that spawned his black hole theory.

Chaos theory made me see that prediction was absurd, that what was expected of me was not necessarily what I would deliver and that, like patterns of cream swirling until incorporated into a mug of refilled coffee, I too could move beyond the constraining, confining boundaries of North Delta and all that it represented. We helped each other to understand that we were operating in molds and that we needed to break out of them if we were ever going to be happy. Lynde bore the heavy weight of expectation which was precisely what I felt I lacked, just as I had freedoms that she couldn't fathom. My parents didn't necessarily expect me to go to university, though they were happy that I did.

Growing up in a suburb meant that I'd been accustomed to luxuries like mattresses and indoor heating; I didn't take well to sleeping outdoors. There was the wind, the chill and the sand's constant interference. We'd light candles and they'd blow out. Eventually, we found some good spots in Stanley Park that were relatively sheltered. We'd create barricades with Lynde's mom's old blankets but we'd still end up cold and wet when the dew fell and the mist came. Sometimes we sat up against the giant logs scattered across the beaches. Sometimes we'd lean against each other, back to back, encased in jackets and scarves. We never gave a thought to safety. With our grand intellectual undertakings, we were so beyond such pedestrian concerns. Besides, on nights we spent at the beach, the world seemed beautiful and pure. However illusory our perception, we always felt protected. And anyway, nothing beat waking up at dawn on Second Beach.

With our bodies almost crunchy from the cold, it was hard to stand up. Having to pee was frustrating as I had to wait until I was able to unfold my crossed legs, stand up, stretch and wander into the bush. Yet the stiffness made me feel alive. There was nothing better than being alone with Lynde, on the beach, in downtown Vancouver at five in the

morning. Five was sacred time. Even night owls are usually gone from the streets by then, and the early risers aren't quite up yet. At 5 AM, two high school girls from North Delta could own the world for a little while.

To us, North Delta seemed to be nowhere.
MARK MUSHET
PHOTO

I guess that was what made the next part hard. There was a freedom, a triumph about those mornings. There was a sense of survival. We lived life the way we wanted to. We did not confine ourselves to square bedrooms in rectangular houses. We broke loose from the social norms that dictate that sleeping happens on mattresses in suburbs. Taking the 312 back to the land of conformity was torturous and seemed beneath us.

The pit in my stomach would ache from the second we took the escalators down to the platform at Granville Station. Going home meant hurting. I was a sensitive teen and I carried my anxiety in my belly.

We took turns at being the voice of reason. Lynde was as sensitive as I was and sometimes she was the one whose stomach hurt. One time she burst into tears and collapsed into a fetal position right on the Burrard Street sidewalk and I cradled her for a long time before we both decided that we simply could not get on that

Architect's drawing of Delta Shoppers Mall on Scott Road, a five-minute walk from where I grew up. By the time I came along, the Pay'n'Save was an Extra Foods. The mall is now gone. DELTA ARCHIVES 2004–3–72

SkyTrain and go back. We knew we only had so many opportunities to spend all night and all day and all of the next night doing whatever we felt like and the longer we stayed away, the harder it was to go back.

For the most part, we knew that we wouldn't be able to come back at night if we didn't show up for school during the day so that 312 bus ride home was a sacrifice we were willing to endure.

The SkyTrain stations became progressively more bland the nearer we came to Scott Road Station. We could trace the building dullness that culminated, we believed, in North Delta. That was the climax of boring. Getting on the 312 and going back up over the bump and up the steep hill and right on 96th Avenue, down through the residential areas, the sleepiness and predictability was more than we could stand.

Last time I drove through North Delta, I decided, for fun, to take the road down to Scott Road Station. The bump is gone now. This generation of North Delta kids will have a smooth bus ride and that makes me sad.

The Summer of Expo

The summer of 1986 was known across the Lower Mainland as the summer of Expo. Expo officials had estimated that somewhere between 5 and 6 million people would show up for the event. In fact, about four times that number came. According to my mom, there is a direct correlation between this huge turnout and a speech that US President Reagan delivered the previous summer. A bunch of American tourists had gone to Italy on a cruise ship and the ship was hijacked by terrorists, and Reagan announced that Americans travelling abroad were basically on their own, security-wise.

Regardless of their motives for coming to Vancouver, they came en masse. People slept in their rental cars in ditches on the side of the road. That spring, my mom opened the house for business. Other than a brief stint at a Danish bakery, this was her first foray into the Canadian workforce. She, like many Canadians in the Lower Mainland — particularly mothers who worked from home — became self-employed as the owner and operator of her own bed & breakfast.

Office towers, parking garages and shopping malls blossomed all over Vancouver under Bill Bennett and Bill Vander Zalm's Social Credit governments. Meanwhile, renters in the Downtown Eastside and near the Expo site were evicted and their homes were renovated to accommodate the massive influx of tourists. Everywhere, even North Delta, was abuzz in a way that even I, at ten years old, could feel. Depending on politics, jobs and housing, people were either pro-Expo or really, really against it.

Mom painted the house. Dad worked long hours. Mom designed a menu for her guests. Dad worked long hours. Mom did a promotional commercial with Shell Busey, whose *Home Improvements* show was by then an established segment on BCTV's Saturday morning news program, for Delta Cablevision. Dad worked long hours. Looking back, it makes sense that Mom scolded him about the green shag rug that they talked about replacing ever since they bought the house five years earlier. Dad shrugged, not because he was indifferent but because he was tired. He wanted her to deal with it. She wanted a team effort. They sipped wine, tapping a little more from the cardboard carton every once in a while. The room filled with cigarette smoke. I listened at the door, humming along to the Paul Simon record my dad put on the player. *Graceland*.

Tourists came. Some of them wanted to eat dinner with us, upstairs. My mom gave her best, sometimes offering to drive her guests to the Expo site or out to UBC for a conference that was rather ill-timed. I barely saw her that summer, unless I tagged along with her in the car or on a shopping trip to Costco, a place that had mayonnaise jars that were even bigger than the ones at Extra Foods.

In Denmark, she had been the breadwinner. My parents met young, my mom still in high school, my dad fulfilling the manda- tory six months of military service required by the government. He was a switchboard operator in the Danish Navy. They moved in together. Then they moved away together, from Fredericia, a tiny town on the Mainland, to Copenhagen, the urban metropo- lis. Mom worked as a nurse in a psychiatric ward. Dad went to school. Mom was promoted. Dad became an apprentice. Even when Dad finished school, Mom's hours never decreased. Then they had me.

Knowing what I know now of the woman who bore me and raised me, I find it hard to understand that she would quit that job — that lifestyle — to move across the Atlantic, across the second largest country in the world, to the west coast of Canada to be a stay-at-home mom in North Delta. My mom has since adapted the story to reflect the logic of biological clocks: a house with a wraparound yard in a safe neighbourhood with enough time to care for a family was not some theoretical dream, it was instinct.

When I went to Denmark, my cousin Ulla, my dad's sister's daughter, who is ten years older than me and who came to visit us in the summer of 1982, showed me her photo album. We looked through the pages. I was struck by how often we were at lakes and in the mountains. We had family visit from Denmark every sum- mer and my mom made every effort to take them on road trips and camping trips and fishing trips and sailing trips. We saw Lake Louise and Banff and Salmon Arm and Harrison Hot Springs. We saw the Cascade mountains, Winthrop, Leavenworth, Port Townsend. We saw Osoyoos, Keremeos and Kelowna. In the pho- tos, she looked tired and exhilarated and so very very young.

The summer of Expo had profound ramifications for all of North Delta. On September 22, 1986, the Alex Fraser Bridge opened, linking North Delta with Richmond and New Westminster via Lulu Island. Crossing the main channel of the Fraser River, the Alex Fraser Bridge was acclaimed for being the longest suspension

bridge in the world, with a 465-metre main span. The stay cables radiate from two tall concrete towers, founded on large steel pipe piles of similar length. The deck is concrete, laid on steel plate girders. Originally the six-lane deck was restricted to four lanes, the outer lanes being reserved for cyclists and pedestrians. It only took about a year before the bridge had generated sufficient traffic to justify opening all six lanes to vehicles. Pedestrians and cyclists were moved outside the cables. The bridge was named for a politician who had recently died, the former Minister of Highways in the provincial government. My family, along with many other North Delta folks, celebrated the completion of the Alex Fraser Bridge by walking across it the day before it was opened to car traffic. Like most of our neighbours, my parents put a bumper sticker on their car that said, "Take the Fraser over the Fraser." To my dad the bridge meant no more taking the bus for almost two hours each way. To my mom, the bridge meant we had to get a second car. To the rest of North Delta, it meant that we were that much closer to fulfilling our potential — a new artery to the city would open up and we would, by proxy, become more cosmopolitan.

In North Delta, everyone said that the city was coming. Con-

Expo 86 and the construction of the Alex Fraser Bridge linking North Delta and Annacis Island changed my hometown forever. DELTA ARCHIVES 1997–14–4

struction was at an all-time high. Henry's Chinese–Canadian Restaurant had its best year ever. The guys who worked on the Alex Fraser Bridge were regular customers, coming to Henry's in the morning for the $1.95 breakfast. Yes: a full breakfast for one dollar and ninety-five cents.

When I asked Elaine's mom, Cecile, how they did this, she explained that eggs come in large, medium, small. Then laughed and told me that at Henry's they used peewee. And the bacon was sliced extra thin. But still. They had to serve a lot of breakfasts to support the family . . . and they did.

North Delta continues to have its charms, especially for young families, and new neighbourhoods continue to go up. MARK MUSHET PHOTO

So the construction guys would get two full breakfasts and tell Cecile and Henry theirs was the best diner around. It was. Henry still talks about the underwater surveyor hired by the contractors on the Alex Fraser Bridge. He was over six feet tall and had a boss who paid for his tab at the diner. Every day, he'd eat a double breakfast, two hamburger steaks for lunch and dinner for four at night.

When Cecile talks about him, she still gasps at the idea of two hamburger steaks, each one the size of a shoe, and one man ordering dinner for four.

Cecile and Henry worked seven days a week, fourteen-hour days for seventeen years. The last few years, they took a half day

off on Sundays. Expo year was the first year that made it seem worthwhile. They had three kids at home. There were a lot of things they missed out on in order to provide North Delta with chicken chow mein and those coveted (and dearly missed) strawberry milkshakes. Cecile, even now, almost fifteen years after they sold the business, shows me how her feet have protrusions from standing for so many hours of so many days and years. Henry tells me he still runs into customers when he goes to Save-On-Foods and they always ask the same thing: When are you going to open another one?

"Why would I do that?" Henry shakes his head. Yet it's clear that he's flattered by his fans. The Yongs, it could be said, lived the Canadian dream. They came with nothing, worked like crazy for years and years and eventually sold the place to developers who demolished the cafe and turned it into an Esso station. Overnight, this allowed Cecile and Henry to retire comfortably. Elaine, who is the youngest, had already graduated by the time her parents sold the diner. She likes to joke that she knows the value of a dollar because she spent her childhood peeling her weight in potatoes. The thing is, it's not a joke. She did peel her weight in potatoes — many times over.

When you go to the corner of 80th and Scott Road now, the Esso station looks comfortable on that corner, across from the 7–11 and the lot that used to be Delta Shoppers Mall. Esso looks like a part of the landscape. But when Henry and Cecile opened the diner, they tell me, the other three corners of that intersection were bush and undeveloped lots.

Because of all the damage the world has suffered in the search for gas and oil — the wars that have been fought, the assault on the environment, multinational corporate domination and even the traffic congestion problem that make the South Fraser Perimeter Road seem like such a good idea — it might be unpopular to see Esso as the good guys. There are, in fact, so many reasons to hate Esso that it's nearly impossible to think of them as what they were to the Yongs: saviours. The best thing that can happen to small Canadian business owners is being bought out by a big American business franchise.

If that is true, my nostalgia is misplaced. I was sad when Henry's closed. I miss it. Lots of people miss it. It was easy to be happy for Henry and Cecile, for Elaine and Cecilia and Henry Jr. who, even though they were all fully grown by then, would get to see their parents outside of those four walls in daylight hours. They would get to go on trips together — as far as Europe, as close as New Westminster. These are things that had not happened for two decades.

My sadness was not for the Yongs. They deserved to travel, to live in a bigger house and to buy the home karaoke unit they wanted. They were free. That was great. I'd even call it triumphant. At the time, I almost wanted to thank Esso for coming to the corner of 80th and Scott Road. Almost.

It's the landscape that saddens me, and it makes no sense. You would think that a 7-11 is superior to an empty, undeveloped lot. Undeveloped lots don't provide sugary slushy drinks or chocolate bars. To anyone with taste buds and some change in their pocket, it would seem like a no-brainer.

What troubles me is something that is harder to put my finger on. It's not development as such. It's the kind of development. North Delta has changed. It went from strip malls and little Ma-and-Pa-owned corner stores where people knew each other (however superficially) to multi-function stores with nationwide television commercials. When I walk down Scott Road now, it's hard to ignore all of the signs that conjure well-known jingles. Now that there's a Cactus Club, a Moxie's, a Keg, an Earls and a Taco Bell, it feels like Scott Road could be anywhere in the Lower Mainland, anywhere in BC, anywhere in Western Canada. North Delta is no longer the North Delta that Lynde, Elaine and I were so desperate to escape. It has become a generic mixture of new-fangled restaurant chains, megastores and discount outlets. I thought I wouldn't care what happened to North Delta. However much I claimed to hate the place, however begrudgingly I admitted it, North Delta was home.

After the Yongs retired from Henry's Chinese–Canadian Restaurant, their kids started bugging them to move to the city. Elaine and I had the same conversation over and over. She'd argue that they could afford to move. I'd agree and add to the argument that my mom could afford to move away too if she wanted. We'd project our desires for them onto them and inevitably conclude that there must be something about living in North Delta that they liked. I decided to ask Cecile point-blank one day. After all, both of Elaine's older siblings had married and moved to Vancouver. Cecile has grandkids in the city. It seemed like a reasonable question.

She looked me in the eye and said she liked Vancouver just fine but there was nowhere to park.

I thought about this for a moment and was almost placated by her certainty. But eventually, I objected. Really? That's the answer? Parking?

Yes, she said. She didn't like having to circle the block. She liked knowing that if she wanted oranges or chicken, she could get in her car, drive to Save-On-Foods and find a spot out front.

Then she added that North Delta was home.

Sport Fishing For the Athletically Challenged

My parents, who had waited five years for their immigration papers, were ecstatic when my dad finally landed a job with a British company that had an office in Vancouver. A couple of my dad's work colleagues had bought houses in North Delta, which made that seem like a good idea. I've since wondered what might have happened if my family had settled in a more prominently immigrant neighbourhood. All I can think now is that it just wouldn't have suited us. My parents were firm believers in integration and cultural immersion. And so we strove to become a typical Delta family.

Around the time of the strip-mallification of the land, social engineers decided to make Delta and Surrey into a grid. Streets went north to south, avenues east to west. We lived on 118A Street which meant that we were on a cul-de-sac one street off of a connector, 118th Street. The grid system is impressively easy to understand.

My parents tried their best to do what Delta families did. On sunny summer days, we went to Kennedy Heights for ice cream at the Big Scoop, the first ice cream place in Delta. For a treat, we went to the Sea Shanty, a fish'n'chips place in Nor-Del. On Sunday afternoons, the kids on our North Delta block used to invite my dad and me to join them for street hockey or softball. Neither of us wanted to, and I admired my dad's clever excuse to stay inside. He

River Road.

DAN BUSHNELL

PHOTO

blamed being from Denmark and said he didn't know the games people played here: that people in Denmark play badminton or soccer. His ignorance of the rules would slow everyone down.

Instead, on weekends my dad took me to New Westminster Quay or Granville Island Market to shop for the meal he was responsible for — the one that cost twice as much and left the kitchen twice as messy. He'd point our pastel yellow Ford LTD north onto Highway 91, and head over the Alex Fraser Bridge, his Elton John tape playing. We'd sing along to "I Guess That's Why They Call It the Blues." Far away from our sporty neighbours, we were actually pretty cool. I always liked going for drives with my dad because he brought snacks. There were mints in the glove compartment or chocolates in the side pocket of the door, little treasures stashed away, waiting for me to find them.

At the market, Dad and I weren't the dweebs who couldn't catch or swing or throw. We were people of refined taste who knew the difference between gouda and gruyère, between vine-ripened and sun-dried. In the privacy of the car, Dad admitted that he was no good at baseball or football or hockey, that he just wasn't interested. Maybe it was his attempt not to embarrass me in front of the athletic crowd. I sighed, relieved that he wouldn't witness his only child being picked last.

But then my dad had a sporting epiphany. His boss paid for a company fishing trip to an artificially-stocked lake north of Prince Rupert. It was the dude ranch of sport fishing, and he came home thrilled. He said he'd found the perfect sport for people like us, and showed us pictures of pasty executives reeling in trout after trout.

My mom argued that fishing was not a sport. It was like she was reading my mind.

I was skeptical all the way to Canadian Tire. Dad picked up a cart at the entrance, bypassed basketballs and hockey sticks and disappeared into the sport-fishing aisle. Mom and I veered off to look at perennials and lawnmowers and slug poison. We found him twenty minutes later, silent and contemplative, teetering over bobbers, hooks and lines. The cart held a tackle box, colourful lures and three rods. Mom switched hers for a sprinkler.

That summer, I turned eleven. In the spirit of achieving this new outdoorsy vision for ourselves, we adopted a dog from the SPCA. Cinder, an Australian blue heeler, needed plenty of exercise. My dad and I were responsible for walking and caretaking. My mom maintained that living with animals was barbaric, that the Vikings did it to stay warm but that we had central heating.

She didn't often come with Cinder, my dad and me to Deas Island to fish in the Fraser River. But we quickly became dedicated athletes, spending weeknights talking about how we'd prepare our first big catch. Maybe parsley. Maybe lemon butter and dill.

Dad and I weren't just in it for the potential culinary rewards; we blossomed into serious sportspeople. We weren't fanatical. We didn't get up early. We knew nothing about salmon. We talked about getting worms but decided it would be a hassle. We didn't pack a bunch of equipment — not even a cooler. Instead, we agreed that the biggest priority was to enjoy ourselves.

We went sporadically on sunny Sunday afternoons for over a year and never caught anything. Some days I didn't even have a hook on my line, just a sinker. It was heavier, and made me feel like my cast was improving. My dad stood at the side of the river, expertly balanced, smoking as he cast his line out further than mine. We were too far away from each other to have a real conversation. We nodded back and forth. Cinder watched. It was perfect.

Twenty years later, when I actually experienced catching a fish, I wondered what would have happened if we'd reeled one in. We didn't have a club or even a knife with us. I couldn't imagine my father carefully placing his Ray-Bans in his shirt pocket to hit a fish over the head with a river rock.

The Danish Dream

Although my mom worked as a psychiatric nurse in Denmark, my parents moved to North Delta for a different life. In Denmark, they would have both had to work outside the home. My mom's new life in this foreign country meant that she would not have to work the hectic schedule that was required of her in Denmark. My dad's work schedule here would involve extremely long hours but, for both of them, that seemed a reasonable trade-off. The plan, as he explains it now, was that he would make money and she would take care of the home — a plan that worked for many couples in North Delta and suburbs across North America — but not a plan that bolstered my parents' relationship or their individual self-esteem. The suburban dream is a powerful one and, after years of striving — of applying for Canadian jobs, then applying for immigration, then applying for a mortgage — they achieved their goal only to realize, as many couples did across North America, that it wasn't what they wanted.

During my elementary years, my mom spent her days cooking, grocery shopping, gardening, cleaning and ironing, and when it was all done, she started over again. The world was supposed to have gotten bigger — that is why one moves across the Atlantic and across Canada: for adventure and excitement, the outdoors and interesting new friends — yet her days, for the most part, consisted of a boxy house with a two-door garage and a wraparound yard and everyone in her life assuming that she was fulfilled.

Her social network involved the checkout line at the K-Mart, the checkout line at Extra Foods, teachers at my school, Danes they knew through the Danish church, and relatives who visited from Denmark. I look back now and wonder how someone so politically opinionated — who taught herself to read English by forcing her way through the Vancouver Sun every morning — could get by without sparring partners or debate clubs. My dad's suggestion was that she make friends with the women who lived on our block. A good idea in theory, but in practice this was an extremely difficult thing for a socialist feminist to do in a culture where most people either supported Bill Vander Zalm or didn't care. This was a neighbourhood in which composting was frowned upon, press-on nails were normal, and Sunday barbeques and street hockey were requirements. Immigration is an isolating experience. This is especially true for those who strive to take part in the mainstream. There is no undoing the past. Wherever one goes, one carries the weight of where one comes from — customs, language, attitudes and expectations. It is impossible to keep up with the Joneses when you don't have a clue what the Joneses are doing or why.

My parents' divorce was inevitable. Growth, by definition, requires pain. Movement, by definition, requires leaving things behind. My dad still speculates over how it happened. What went wrong? They loved each other; they loved me. We had a nice home on a nice street in a nice neighbourhood. I spent years blaming North Delta for the demise of our family unit but what happened, in my opinion, was that my dad felt a huge burden of responsibility to provide for his family and so he threw himself into his work. The other way of looking at it — one I relate to from personal experience, and I blame my genes — is that my dad is a workaholic and he did not know how to prioritize his family until it was too late. He learned the hard way that people who don't feel valued leave.

What my mom needed to do — and eventually would do — was to become a self-employed success, a woman with a good retirement plan, a paid-off mortgage and an investment portfolio, a woman who could enjoy the pleasure of a male suitor on her own terms, not because she was financially reliant. What my dad needed to do — and eventually would do — was to see the world, to become a bonafide globetrotter and a man of many languages, someone who could be comfortable anywhere and strike up a conversation with anyone.

What also happened, in my opinion, is that my mom was not accomplishing her life's work in raising me and being domestic. The other way of looking at it — one I relate to from personal experience, and I blame my genes for this, too — is that my mom doesn't know how to feel supported or ask for help. In order to do what she needs to do, my mom needs to do things alone.

Regardless of which explanations seem reasonable, my dad moved out in 1991, though the papers weren't signed until years later. I was fourteen at the time. My mom became a realtor and sold the family home herself. My dad, who had worked diligently for a decade, received a promotion and become an expatriate. The deal was that the company would pay him more and he would, in exchange, make himself so mobile that he could be uprooted within two weeks. That is what happened. Before he knew it, he went from a familiar (if tense) home in North Delta to a one-bedroom apartment in Johannesburg, South Africa, where he knew no one. Mom and I moved from Nor-Del near Delta Shoppers

Mall to a townhouse complex in Sur-Del, across the street from the Sikh temple, and behind the Cheers Pub and Scottsdale Mall.

We lived in a rectangle of townhouses with a rectangular shared courtyard in the back. From my room I could see a cluster of mature trees, tokens that had been left alone to remind us of what was here before the land had changed hands and zoning. There was a little playground off to one corner with a sandbox and a tire swing. I stayed in my room and listened to REM.

I continued to blame North Delta because it was there and it was easy and because I loved my parents and didn't want to take sides. My dad was the only dad I knew who had worn a suit to work, since most of the other dads were in trades. My mom was the only mom I knew who had short nails and carpentry skills. At the time, I didn't know why we were so weird; I just knew that we were, and surely people who feel weird eventually burn out.

Other Weirdos

As a seven-year-old, on my walks to and from Richardson Elementary, I developed a fear of the woman everyone referred to as The Walking Lady. I'd pass her on my way to and from school and I knew the stories. Because it seemed that all she did all day was walk up and down the streets of North Delta, rumours circulated. Maybe this was mostly in my demographic, but her tanned loose skin and her purple halter top and shorts made her a fascinating character worthy of celebrity. The most popular theories were that she had lost a son and wandered the streets in search of his spirit and that she had cancer and if she stopped walking, she would die. I was afraid of the way she mumbled to herself and wouldn't make eye contact. She was ghostly and reminded me of a hamster in one of those transparent plastic orbs.

I was also afraid of Burns Bog. The bog, the playground kids said, could suck people in just like those quicksand scenes in B-movies. I imagined making one false step and being doomed. Surjinder told me a story she had heard about a tractor that had gotten stuck in the quicksand, the driver only escaping by grabbing onto branches and lifting himself out using a tree as a catapult. The kids said there were venus flytrap plants, which I was also afraid of. It is true that there are spots with quicksand and flesh-eating plants in the bog, but the reality of these phenomena is far less dramatic — the quicksand is practically inaccessible to pedestrians, and the plants eat only insects.

I was afraid of the black bears that used to come up into the neighbourhoods from the bog in search of garbage. But after the Alex Fraser Bridge created a barrier for them, they stuck to the other side of the bridge and their population dwindled. Bog bears, which are genetically different from black bears, are gone now too. At the time, I thought this was good — I didn't like the idea of bears wandering the streets at night.

One summer, when I was fourteen, my friends and I found a motorcycle in the bog. It was actually a moped or scooter, but we called it a motorcycle and felt every bit as cool as Meatloaf while riding it. And after my friend's dad fixed it, we rode it along the old train tracks that trace the border between the bog and North Delta. It had been a while since the train stopped running; all that was left was a path. We rode it every single day that summer.

When high school started and we graduated from Burnsview Junior High to North Delta Senior Secondary, the bog was no longer a place for me or my friends. Overnight, it had become unsafe for geeks and weirdos. High school ushered in a new era and the bog became the place to go to get drunk, have sex, do drugs and just hang out. Even for the barely to moderately cool, the bog was *the* Friday- and Saturday-night destination.

By time I was fifteen, the bog became the place I only heard about when I eavesdropped on conversations about the weekend. While I had been home on Saturday nights watching *Golden Girls* and curling my hair, so-and-so had made it to second base or stolen a bottle of vodka from their parents' liquor cabinet and gotten *way hammered, man.*

If I went out at all, it was to the Yongs'. Cecilia, Elaine's older sister, was a whiz with the VCR and usually taped the week's highlights — *Scooby Doo, Love Connection* or *Anne of Green Gables.* The Yong family basement was where we spent most of our time, usually with some kind of snack — wontons or jujubes — and wrapped in blankets. The Yongs had an assortment of blankets, the best of which was a blue and green striped one that we dubbed the Snake Blanket because of its stripes and also because once engulfed in that number, the wearer was almost certain to fall into a deep slumber and lie around like a coiled snake in the jungle.

We'd watch cartoons and have conversations about things that simultaneously meant everything and nothing. We wondered why Fred always chose Daphne over Velma and we dissected *Scooby Doo* plots, analyzing them for their realism or what the villains represented. We used the villains as code names for everyone at school we didn't like. We also wondered what it would be like to live on Prince Edward Island, or meet Chuck Woolery or guess the right price on *The Price Is Right*. What else was there to do? We weren't into sports. We weren't into music. We didn't have hobbies and we didn't have cash. We didn't drink. We didn't do drugs. We didn't smoke. Maybe we should have. The natural by-product of our condition was to belittle everyone we knew and many we didn't.

We were North Delta girls, and that was a tragic fate. White Rock girls lived in nice houses off the beach. Surrey girls had their notorious reputations. There were jokes dedicated to them, acknowledging their importance and providing them with a stereotype to either inhabit or resist. Being from North Delta meant being from a whole other stratosphere of blandness, and we knew it. As an adult who has since run into old classmates, I now know that there were other weirdos stranded in their parents' basements trying to create their own fun, but we didn't know that at the time.

Elaine and I had lots of sources of entertainment but the best was prank calling. Those were the days before call display. We'd call the pay phone at Delta Shoppers Mall or look up unusual names in the phone book, but soon we grew more mature in our pursuits. Prank calling random people in North Delta was one thing. Artistically speaking, it ranked fairly low. In our refinement, we became more interested in trickier executions, like calling infomercial hotlines. Our favourite was Miracle Blade. It could slice through a beer can and then a tomato. Amazing. It took all night to get the script just right. Then it took skill and concentration. I tried to dial the number myself, but every time my fingers made their way across the keypad, my whole body would shake with suppressed laughter and my bladder would threaten to burst. I passed the phone to Elaine, who had either been practicing or was simply more talented than me.

With a straight face, Elaine told them she was a jeweller and was wondering whether Miracle Blade could cut diamonds. I was hunched over on the couch, my teeth clenching the Snake Blanket, my hands squeezing a cushion, desperate not to make a sound or pee my pants. They couldn't answer the diamond-cutting question and informed her that she'd have to call head office.

By my last year in high school, counsellors, teachers and other well-meaning adults insisted that I would one day look back upon those years as being the best of my life. I tried my best to convince them that they were delusional, living in a *Beverly Hills 90210* world where cheerleading and football were fun and inclusive activities. I called their propaganda. I couldn't afford to believe that life would only get worse. I hadn't escaped yet and I wasn't convinced it would be an easy feat.

That same year, the first Starbucks opened on Scott Road. Lynde, Elaine and I, with our very dignified seventeen-year-old palates, rejected the idea of lattes for the masses. We preferred the Euro Café. Starbucks was not the first big city chain that came to our neighbourhood; it was just another one on what seemed like an endless list of American companies selling products that everyone seemed thrilled with. To us, it was the same old Lumberland parking lot serving the same old soccer moms a new-fangled four-dollar version of the same old drink.

Starbucks intensified the depressive nature of the North Delta landscape. The Euro Café only managed to stay open for another year or so. The place was most empty except for the owners' friends who played pool in the back. Starbucks, however, was packed from the day of its grand opening.

Getting Out

Graduation was supposed to mark the attainment of freedom. It didn't. It was infuriatingly anti-climatic. My mom did not help to minimize my general disillusionment. What she actually said was something like: *You need a plan. No daughter of mine is going to sit around and watch television between shifts at the cafeteria.*

Well, yeah. I didn't even like TV. What I heard was something different, something that signified that the end was near, if it hadn't already arrived.

You need a plan. Maybe get a retail job. You could work your way into management. Eventually, you could save for a down payment. You could buy yourself an apartment or a townhouse or something. Maybe move a little further into the valley. Real estate is cheaper in Langley and Cloverdale. Get married. Have kids. Be normal.

What I heard was that she did not believe any more than I did that I could leave North Delta. What I heard was that I should accept my fate, be a good person, ask neither too much nor too little, work hard, save, and perpetuate the status quo. My mom never said these things but I was sensitive and I heard things that weren't said. We also didn't talk much in those days. It was a busy time for her. She was in school, trying to figure out a way to survive on her own, trying to navigate her way as a single mother in a culture that was not her own, in a place that was home now but not totally. She had a Canadian passport but she still had an accent.

It was a lonely time. Lynde had gone off tree planting and Elaine was getting ready to go to university. I knew I would not be accepted with my transcript as it was and I also knew I did not want to go to Kwantlen College up the street and face another year or more with all the same faces I knew from high school — especially on my own dime. I toodled around our townhouse for a week, mostly hiding in my room, listening to REM on repeat. I needed a plan and did not have one. So I answered an ad in the back of *The Leader*: "Make big $$$ talking on the phone."

It sounded promising. I passed the interview which consisted of telling my new boss my name and my social insurance number and giving my availability, which was all the time. Before I knew it, I was taking the bus to Scott Road Station, the SkyTrain to Surrey Central and, after a ten-minute walk, three flights of stairs to a fluorescent-lit, dystopian cubicle nightmare.

I sold Grade-A Alberta beef. I had the speech memorized after my first shift and other than the randomness of the phone numbers I dialed, I could predict every hang-up, every tediously awful conversation with prospective meat buyers and every kind-hearted excuse to get off the phone and back to dinner. My boss offered the incentive of six free steaks when we reached our quota. Only one guy in the office, an ex-con who was trying to patch things up with his girlfriend, ever actually won his free steaks. I would have envied his work ethic and enthusiasm if I hadn't hated the place so much. Selling beef over the phone was, I felt at the time, hitting an all-time low. I didn't even meet the quota to earn minimum wage. I was pretty sure this was God-Santa's way of evening the score for what we did to the poor folks at the Miracle Blade hot-line. Three weeks later, I got on a plane and left North Delta and made the vow — that I would break — never to come back.

Cheap Land

I knew a well-meaning realtor. She was also my landlord and I liked her, even though she evicted me so that she could reno-vate the house and charge the next tenants a lot more rent. She claimed to know what my problem was: my lack of home own-ership. According to her, Vancouver's soaring real-estate market means that first-time homeowners, especially women who want to live alone, should not focus on trying to find a place in Vancouver proper and should, instead, set their sights on buying real estate in "the valley", meaning Fraser Valley, or the urban sprawl constitut-ing everything even further away than North Delta.

When I told her that I'm a Vancouverite in my heart and that the city makes me happy, she reasoned that it would be better for my future to move out of my Vancouver rental suite and put a down payment on a place of my own, even if it meant spending a couple of hours per day commuting. She told me I would get used to it, that nowadays the suburbs were changing and looked urban, that I could hang out at Starbucks and Chapters and Earls and Cactus Club and it would be just like living in the city.

What I couldn't tell her, because she was so adamant, is that Starbucks and Chapters and Cactus Club do not a city make. Yes, one can indeed move all of the big stores and American chains into Canadian suburbs. We can and we do. This is the new land-scape for places like North Delta. But no matter how many bright shining new plazas and outlet stores and restaurants with exten-sive martini lists, these exurbs are not cities.

The last time I drove through the valley, I saw handfuls of "city centres", swarms of recognizable places, conveniently located around parking lots, designed for drivers and people chasing the home ownership dream. In Abbotsford I even saw a sign, a new city slogan: "Welcome to Abbotsford, a city in the country." I couldn't help but wonder if that is what Abbotsford, a place with its own unique history and population, truly wants to be.

These placeless places, these development sites that boast "urban condo living" have become a kind of landscape unto themselves. In these places you can wander around, comforted by predictability. Expectations are met. It's like being at Tim Horton's or McDonald's, knowing precisely what you are getting. Without any kind of natural obstacle or wonder to distract, you don't even have to think about the history of the land. History becomes obsolete; you can be lulled into accepting a world where everything is new and sparkly and American.

North Delta's new land- scape consists of strip malls populated by franchise outlets and chain restaurants. MARK MUSHET PHOTO

Alongside these new metropoles, there are herons aching to go home. There are cranes and shrews and deer and bears that are lost. There are ghost fields of yarrow and goldenrod, longing to repopulate the concrete-covered landscape. There are legacies and stories of the people who came before. Wetlands are easy to drain. Dense, rich histories are easy to pave over.

Even if it weren't a matter of environmental ethics, I would still rather spend the rest of my life renting in a neighbourhood that I like, where I like to drink coffee, eat lunch, buy produce or have a random conversation with a stranger, than sign myself on to a piece of land that's an hour's commute away. It's a cultural prefer-

ence, a realization that I enjoy places that have identities, however complex.

It is difficult to express this viewpoint to my parents who, each in their own way, emphasize the importance of home ownership, investment, getting ahead in a country that was gracious enough to open its doors to us. My parents have been more than willing to sacrifice abstract ideas like culture in favour of pragmatic things like interest rates. Unless you go to the theatre all the time, you don't need to live close to one, they argue. And in many ways, they're right: I do stay home a lot. Why do I want to live in Vancouver, one of the world's most desirable cities, when I rarely leave my apartment?

Searching

Recently I went back to Denmark for a visit. I arrived in Copenhagen and was met by Thomas, my friend from my stay there as a teenager. Thomas whisked me off to the local pub for the very Danish welcome, a few pints of cold Tuborg. A decade earlier, I had left North Delta in the hopes of finding vindication (or some sense of meaning or belonging or whatever it was I was searching for) in Kolding, the small town where my extended family still lives, twenty minutes from the town where both of my parents grew up, the place they left as soon as they could. This time, I wasn't on a quest for vindication. I just wanted to hang out with a friend.

In Copenhagen, across from Thomas, reminiscing about old times, I felt alive and free from the moment I landed in that vibrant city. It was as if the streets, the old buildings, the beautiful parks all had a way of breathing energy into me and fuelling my drive to reconnect with the place I had come from. It was a different Denmark, or perhaps I was different.

Copenhagen, like many European cities, seems like a gathering place for beautiful people. Everyone is (or appears to be) healthy and statuesque. It isn't the kind of random runway beauty that one sometimes sees in North America where, once in a while, at Zellers or Red Lobster, you see someone truly breathtaking. In Copenhagen, it's an overall thing, as if the entire population made a decision a long time ago that no one would ever wear sweatpants or scrunchies or sequins. There is an effortlessness about it, possibly linked to the ubiquitous acceptance of bicycling and walking as primary modes of transportation. Everyone has rosy cheeks.

Thomas sat me down at Nyhavn, a stretch of pubs and restaurants along Copenhagen's harbourfront, and told me to expect something amazing. He brought back a hot dog — Denmark's most prized junk food — slathered in remoulade, fried onions and pickled cucumbers. There we were, standing in front of the apartment that Hans Christian Andersen called home, long before this part of town became popular and expensive.

I'd found home, I thought. This was where I belonged.

Thomas asked me why I didn't just move back. We tucked ourselves in at yet another sidewalk café for yet another tall glass of Tuborg.

I told him I'd need a job. I'd need an apartment. I made an excuse that my Danish wasn't good enough. Feeling at home here was different from actually making it my home. I knew that.

Thomas pointed out how many Swedes are getting hired all over the place and how much I'd like living in his neighbourhood. He was right. I loved the vintage fashion stores, the funky record shops, the kiosks and that it only took a few days before I started running into the same people out on the streets. Istedgade, where Thomas lives, has a strong sense of community, one that resists gentrification, one that wouldn't support a Starbucks or a Dairy Queen or a Cactus Club.

Copenhagen doesn't have a red light district like Amsterdam does but the part of town that Thomas lives in was, for years, considered a close cousin. Lined with sex shops and strip clubs, coffee shops and wine bars, Istedgade, the main street in the Vesterbro area, was where Thomas and I dedicated ourselves to getting a little drunk that afternoon. It was easy. Practically every street corner offered drink specials and great food.

The shops along Istedgade maintain remnants of their working-class backgrounds. The foundations aren't as solid, the exteriors have undergone recent modernizations. It reminded me of the years I spent living on Vancouver's Main Street, a place that was inherently hip because of the buildings and the people who chose to occupy them. Like Main Street, Istedgade was once replete with funky inexpensive housing, quirky businesses, students, artists, and characters who didn't necessarily feel comfortable in the fancier parts of town.

Most of the apartments along the side streets of Istedgade, including the one Thomas bought five years ago, are tenements. They've been modernized — most have showers — but there are no elevators in the district and no patios or luxurious gardens. There aren't any freestanding houses. The whole area was built with low-income budgets in mind.

It's not surprising that Istedgade, with its now fashionable hipster façade, is still home to Copenhagen's workers, writers, thinkers and queers. Cheap housing is often what creates community and Istedgade is no exception. Since its inception, there's been a strong sense of identity around the one-kilometre street. This is a place that knows itself and vehemently so. During the Nazi occupation of Denmark, the people of this area coined the still-famous slogan, "You can take Rome and Paris — but Stalingrad and Istedgade will never surrender."

Istedgade, the city of my dreams. STEEN L. LARSEN PHOTO

I tell my Danish relatives and my Canadian friends that my heart is Canadian. But stepping off of a plane into a country I haven't even been to for ten years and feeling immediately needed, was the equivalent of a teary-eyed reunion. Though Thomas and I are both considered outsider-renegades of Danish culture (him because he was adopted from a different country, me because I was raised in a different country), we talked at length about Copenhagen's awesomeness.

Thomas wouldn't let up on the idea that I should move to Copenhagen. I was starting to flirt with the idea as well. He argued that since Canada was so close to America, I'd grown up a victim of cultural colonization, an argument that was difficult to refute especially since North Delta had during my visit to Denmark become the Canadian beachhead for Krispy Kreme's planned invasion of my country. He argued that Denmark would

expose me to a different mindset. I could learn about Danish envi-
ronmentalism and about windmill technology. He urged me to
move to a country where I could really fit in and belong and be
valued. He was so adamant that he invited me along to an evening
of networking with some of his friends.

To my delight, they immediately commented that my Danish
was just fine, that they could hear an accent but that these days
every other person in Copenhagen has an accent anyway. How
had I maintained it, they wanted to know, and so I told them that
my parents spoke only Danish to me at home. I told them about
how my parents moved to Vancouver when I was five.

People who live in Copenhagen are notorious for seeing themselves as vastly different from people who live elsewhere in Denmark. One of them interrupted to find out whether I meant "here
as in Copenhagen" and so I told her that that was almost the case
but not quite: "here as in Taastrup." My accent gives me away anyway. It's clear that my parents are from Jutland.

I sometimes forget that distance is an abstract concept. Thirty
minutes of travel in Canada means the difference between Vancouver and North Vancouver, or Downtown Vancouver and
South Vancouver. In Denmark, thirty minutes of travel can
mean an entirely different dialect, building style, landscape and
culture. It takes almost a week to drive across Canada, whereas a
cross-country trip of Denmark takes about three hours. In relative
terms, then, my being from Hoje Taastrup might be the Vancouver equivalent of being from, well, North Delta.

That's when one of Thomas's other friends told me that Taastrup is Denmark's most boring town, that it's all subdivisions and
that nothing interesting ever happens there and nothing ever will.
I couldn't speak. It sounded all too familiar. I took a sip of my
Tuborg.

Then another one broke it down even further and asked whether
I meant Taastrup or Hoje Taastrup, which was something like
making the distinction between Ladner and North Delta. So I
told them: Hoje Taastrup.

There was immediate consensus that my parents did me a huge
favour in moving away, that Hoje Taastrup was the worst place
ever, a true hell on earth.

I wanted to tell them that my parents hadn't actually moved to

Vancouver as I had just said. I wanted to explain that distances are different on my continent, that I grew up in the Canadian equivalent of Hoje Taastrup, and I wanted to know whether they had an expression like *the boonies*, and whether they agreed that *the boonies*, like boredom, is relative and exists on a continuum. Instead, a silent disillusionment came over me as I imagined what my life could have been. Had my parents raised me in Hoje Taastrup, I likely would have had all the same problems I had in North Delta. I would have rebelled against the boredom. I would have felt uninspired by the apathy. I would have skipped school and taken the train into Copenhagen to try to get away just like I had caught the bus out of North Delta. My teen angst might have been no more profound, but there would have been a key difference: I could not have told myself I did not belong there, that I wasn't from there. There would not have been an array of eclectic allies to mirror my own exotic status.

I told Thomas's friends I might take the train out and see the town I could have grown up in. The whole table unanimously agreed that I shouldn't bother, that there was nothing to see. It's just rows and rows of boring seventies-style townhouses, they told

Hoje Taastrup, the Copenhagen suburb where I was born, today. The architecture is different from North Delta's, but the effect is the same. MARINA AGUIAR PHOTO

me, and I conjured images of fluorescent-lit supermarket aisles. North Delta is a place where the streets and avenues are perfectly parallel and perpendicular to each other. It's a grid. Like Hoje Taastrup. And supermarkets.

So why did people live there, I wanted to know. Cheap land, they told me. Houses had been built there as a social experiment when Danish designers were invested in the idea that community is based on our ability to see each other. Townhouses in Hoje Taastrup were built with large windows and shared spaces for children to play and families to spend time. Everyone knew what their neighbours were up to. It was like Bentham's Panopticon, the eighteenth-century prison architecture style in which inmates would not be able to tell whether they were being actively observed or not and would therefore wind up self-policing or co-policing. To me, that kind of living would lead to either indifference or paranoia, both of which would be irksome. Maybe there was something to North Delta's strip malls, and random empty lots and promises of development. Though the houses on my street were almost all the same, big boxy seventies houses with yellow tinted windows next to the front doors, at least the windows were frosted.

I had wanted Copenhagen to be my place. Instead, I had to remind myself that I wasn't Danish in the traditional sense. I had been altered. I was as comfortable — or more comfortable — with Wonder bread and Cheez Whiz and boil-in-a-bag corn as I was with Danish food, a fact that I would not admit to the Danes in front of me, knowing they would grimace in disgust. I was more used to shopping malls and fluorescent lights than I was to buildings that had not changed for centuries. I was tired of seeing pretty people everywhere. I wanted food courts and empty lots, rugged highway construction and restaurants that weren't trendy or even all that clean. I wanted Vancouver; my Vancouver. I wanted to go home. Were I to move to Denmark, I would not belong. I would be a Canadian living a Danish existence. I'd be a hybrid.

Had my parents not moved to North Delta, I might have felt a sense of belonging in Hoje Taastrup. I might have felt as entitled and privileged as the people who marginalize Thomas for his visibly un-Danish ethnicity. I could have been the kind of stock character that we mocked, a fate worse than anything. I would have fit in. I would have had a name everyone could pronounce. I would have enjoyed the same food as everyone else. Everything would have been easy, and I would have hated it.

Nothing is Neutral

The Baha'i scriptures say something about geography being a state of mind. It's more eloquent than that and resonates with me, because when I drove through the streets of North Delta, it surprised me to feel sad. I wasn't supposed to have nostalgia for North Delta. I wasn't supposed to care about Starbucks moving in, about the Krispy Kreme and the drive-through bank minutes away from where my mom lives. Juxtaposed with American fast-food outlets, there's something vaguely authentic about the vacant overgrown lots I grew up with. Now that it's gone, I realize there was something quaint about our Delta Shoppers Mall, our Bosley's Pet Food Store and the corner grocery. I wasn't supposed to care and now I do. I care that the next generation of Deltoids will grow up attached to Taco Bell and the other chains that attempt to make this land the same as any other.

Coming Home

Long after Lynde had moved to the US and Elaine had moved to Toronto, I tagged along on a tour of Burns Bog. A chic urbanite from Montreal taught me about the plants I could have picked and survived on when I was a kid. She taught me that the weeds I used to make bouquets with are called horsetail and they contain silica and you can brush your teeth with the stem of the plant. It's funny. I grew up so close to it. I played in it. I heard stories about it. I rode a moped through it. I walked aimlessly along its edges. But I had never learned much about it.

Apparently, this makes me no different from the next generation of North Delta youth. The Burns Bog Conservation Society teaches thousands of students about the bog. The field-trippers come by the busload from Vancouver, Richmond, New Westminster, even Langley and Chilliwack. I asked about North Delta kids, what they do to learn about the bog. But not North Delta. Delta kids learn about the bog by living close by.

The police officer whose job it is to patrol the land complains

*The famous
Burns Bog
tractor. Only
the top of the
cab hasn't
sunk into
the bog.*
BURNS BOG
CONSERVATION
SOCIETY

that he can't get people to stop illegally dumping things like trucks and car parts in the bog. Once they start sinking into the ground, little can be done. On the tour, I saw the infamous tractor. It's been there since 1972 and even a helicopter can't pull it out. Unlike what I grew up believing, it isn't sinking into a pool of quicksand. It's being enveloped in the bouncy but solid ground. The nature of a bog is to preserve its layers. The kids on the tour, who obviously hadn't grown up with quicksand nightmares and stories of sinking vessels, boldly stomped all over the ground by the tractor. They tugged at it and touched it. One guy pulled out a camcorder. When future generations manage to excavate the tractor and other abandoned artifacts, they will find them in much the same condition they were in when they sank into the bog. I wonder what they will then make of our Dodge Chargers, shopping carts and condom wrappers.

Home Is Just a Story

Going back to North Delta wasn't the problem I thought it would be. I learned (and relearned) that my mom was right about God-Santa and about the value of searching for meaning.

Building a highway over the 9,000-year-old village is wrong, not because development per se is bad but because it is unethical to erase history for future generations who might care.

Burns Bog is indeed the most impressive and expansive raised peat bog in an urban area in the Northern Hemisphere. This sets it apart, but it is linked to wetlands everywhere, just as strip mall landscapes and our desire to live in them are inextricably linked. The conflict (or losing battle) of wetlands *versus* development is much larger than North Delta, spanning most of the globe. Eliza Olson from the Burns Bog Conservation Society showed me (and would show anyone willing to look) a map of the Lower Mainland's wetlands a hundred years ago and one today. When we drive past the PNE now, we might think to ourselves: There used to be a bog here. When we drive along Lougheed Highway in Burnaby or over the Queensborough Bridge in New Westminster, we're driving on land that was bog land not that long ago. And eventually, I imagine, people will be driving along the South Fraser Perimeter Road, or they'll be crossing Alex Fraser Bridge and now and then someone will think to themselves: There used to be a bog here.

What Thomas and I agreed upon as angry teens, that humanity is doomed, that we are headed for extinction, seemed cynical then. We lowered our voices so that our manager and co-workers wouldn't hear us. It made sense that we didn't get along with most of our peers.

Change is inevitable. That there are more people and less space in the Lower Mainland than ever makes sense. This is a great place to be. What we cannot predict — though we can monitor

Eliza Olson of the Burns Bog Conservation Society.

and measure — is the effect that our gathering here will have. How do I say goodbye to a 9,000-year-old village that I never even had a chance to get to know?

I was driving home from North Delta in rush-hour traffic on the Alex Fraser Bridge when I noticed a bumper sticker on the car in front of me. It said: "Where are we going and why am I in this handbasket?"

Acknowledgements

In writing this book, I learned how true it is that history is made up of individual stories. To everyone who let me rummage through your memories, thank you for lending your story to the creation of this artifact.

I would like to thank Daphne Marlatt for encouraging me to tell my story, Gudrun Will for editing and publishing the first install-ment in *Vancouver Review*, and Terry Glavin for seeing that the article was the beginning of a book and for mentoring me through the process. To the organizers and participants of the Sikholars Conference at Stanford University in Spring 2010, I would like to express my sincere gratitude for your encouragement.

A heartfelt thanks to Eliza Olson and everyone at the Burns Bog Conservation Society for tirelessly answering my questions about peat lands and politics, and for the use of the photo of the famous sunken tractor on page 84.

Thanks also to Catharine McPherson and Kathy Bossort at the Delta Archives, for patiently obliging all my strange requests over the past five years, and for providing many of the historical photos used in this book; and to Mark Mushet and Dan Bushnell for their photographic interpretations of Delta and for accompanying me on my return to personal ground zero. Dan, thank you for theoriz-ing Dairy Queen with me.

Many thanks to Rob West for the use of his picture of the 2005 fire on page 27, to Steen L. Larsen for the photo of Istedgade on page 79, and to Marina Aguiar for the use of her photo of Hoje Taastrup on page 81.

Thanks, too, to Rolf Maurer and Stefania Alexandru at New Star Books for seeing what needed seeing and steering me in the right direction.

Finally, and most importantly, to the peers and friends who sup-ported this project from the start, thank you, thank you, thank you.

NEW STAR BOOKS LTD.
107 – 3477 Commercial Street, Vancouver, BC v5n 4e8   CANADA
1574 Gulf Road, No. 1517, Point Roberts, WA 98281   USA
www.NewStarBooks.com   info@NewStarBooks.com

TRANSMONTANUS is edited by Terry Glavin. Editorial correspondence should be sent to 107 – 3477 Commercial Street, Vancouver, BC v5n 4e8   *info@NewStarBooks.com*

Cover by Mutasis.com
Cover photo by Mark Mushet
Typeset at New Star Books
Printed on 100% post-consumer recycled paper
Printed & bound in Canada by Gauvin Press
First printing, June 2010

The publisher acknowledges the financial support of the Government of Canada through the Canada Council and the Department of Canadian Heritage Book Publishing Industry Development Program, and of the Province of British Columbia through the British Columbia Arts Council and the Book Publishing Tax Credit.

LIBRARY AND ARCHIVES CANADA CATALOGUING IN PUBLICATION

Bach, Mette
   Off the highway : growing up in North Delta / Mette Bach.

(Transmontanus 18)
ISBN 978-1-55420-049-8

   1. Bach, Mette — Childhood and youth. 2. North Delta (B.C.) — History. 3. North Delta (B.C.) — Biography.
I. Title. II. Series: Transmontanus 18

FC3849.N62B33 2010   971.1'33   C2010-901740-4